Best·Selling Bazaar PATCHWORK

Compiled and Edited by
Barbara H. Abrelat

Published by Oxmoor House, Inc.
and Leisure Arts, Inc.

Library of Congress Catalog Number: 92-80725
Hardcover ISBN: 0-8487-1092-4
Softcover ISBN: 0-8487-1172-6
Manufactured in the United States of America
Second Printing 1993

Editor-in-Chief: Nancy J. Fitzpatrick
Senior Crafts Editor: Susan Ramey Wright
Senior Editor, Editorial Services: Olivia Wells
Director of Manufacturing: Jerry Higdon
Art Director: James Boone

Best-Selling Bazaar Patchwork

Editor: Barbara H. Abrelat
Editorial Assistant: Roslyn Oneille Hardy
Copy Chief: Mary Jean Haddin
Assistant Copy Editor: Susan Smith Cheatham
Production Manager: Rick Litton
Associate Production Manager: Theresa L. Beste
Production Assistant: Pam Beasley Bullock
Designer: Barbara Ball
Patterns and Illustrations: Karen Tindall Tillery, Melinda Johansson, Carol Loria, Finished Art, Inc.
Senior Photographer: John O'Hagan
Contributing Photographer: Beth Maynor
Photostylist: Katie Stoddard

CONTENTS

Patchwork Pleasures

Cupboard Collection

Happy Patchwork

The joy of stitching pretty patchwork is multiplied when you share your handmade creations with others. That's why, working with designers and bazaar planners from all over the country, we've created a festival of small projects that will make the most of your time and needlework skills.

Because bazaar items must be made quickly, we'll show you the newest time-saving methods. Follow our diagrams for nonstop machine quilting, zip through cutting without templates using a rotary cutter, or create the look of appliqué with stencils. Making small projects is the best way to try these new techniques, and our step-by-step instructions make it easy.

But much as we value saving precious minutes, we also know that you want to be proud of everything you make. Our patchwork bazaar is filled with small items that you will be happy to sell or to give as gifts. Inspired by the rich heritage of traditional patchwork designs, hand-crafted with pleasure, these projects are sure to be bazaar best-sellers.

Patchwork Pleasures

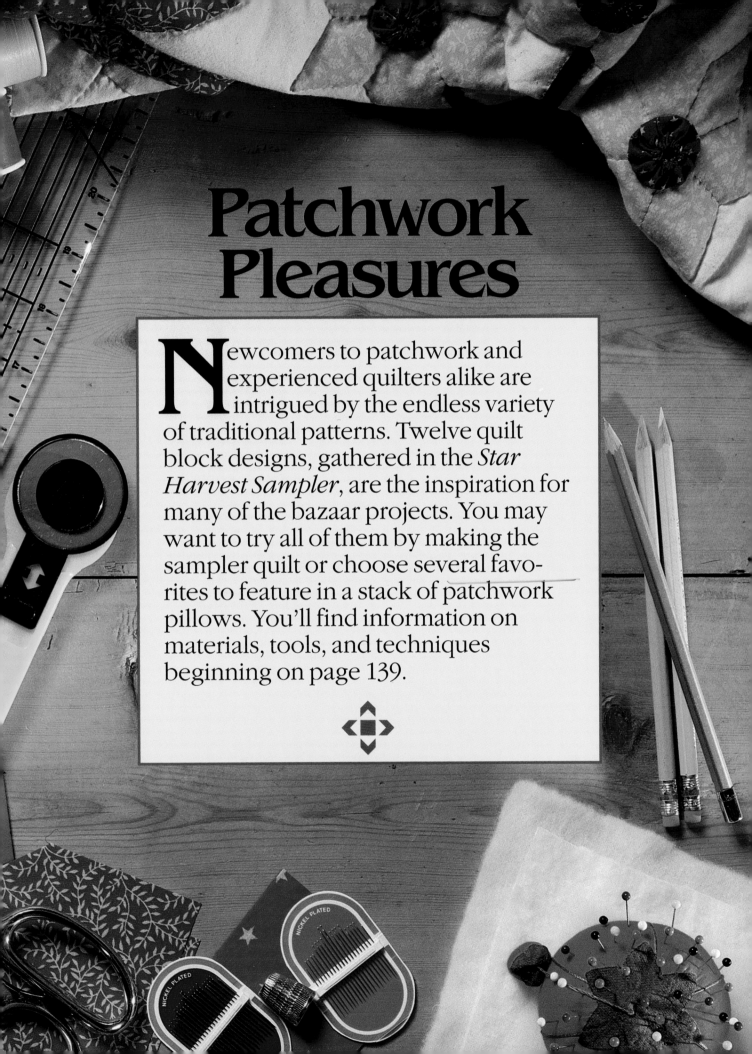

Newcomers to patchwork and experienced quilters alike are intrigued by the endless variety of traditional patterns. Twelve quilt block designs, gathered in the *Star Harvest Sampler*, are the inspiration for many of the bazaar projects. You may want to try all of them by making the sampler quilt or choose several favorites to feature in a stack of patchwork pillows. You'll find information on materials, tools, and techniques beginning on page 139.

8

Star Harvest Sampler Quilt

The *Star Harvest Sampler* quilt features 12 favorite block patterns that will look as great in sophisticated contemporary prints as in comfortable country calicoes. These blocks were chosen to offer a variety of techniques such as freezer-paper appliqué, folded fabric rosebuds, and yo-yo flowers.

The instructions for the blocks have been arranged in order of difficulty, from easy to more challenging. So if you're new to patchwork, you may want to choose some of the first blocks and make them into patchwork pillows before starting on the quilt. Patterns for all of the blocks begin on page 152.

Block Placement Diagram

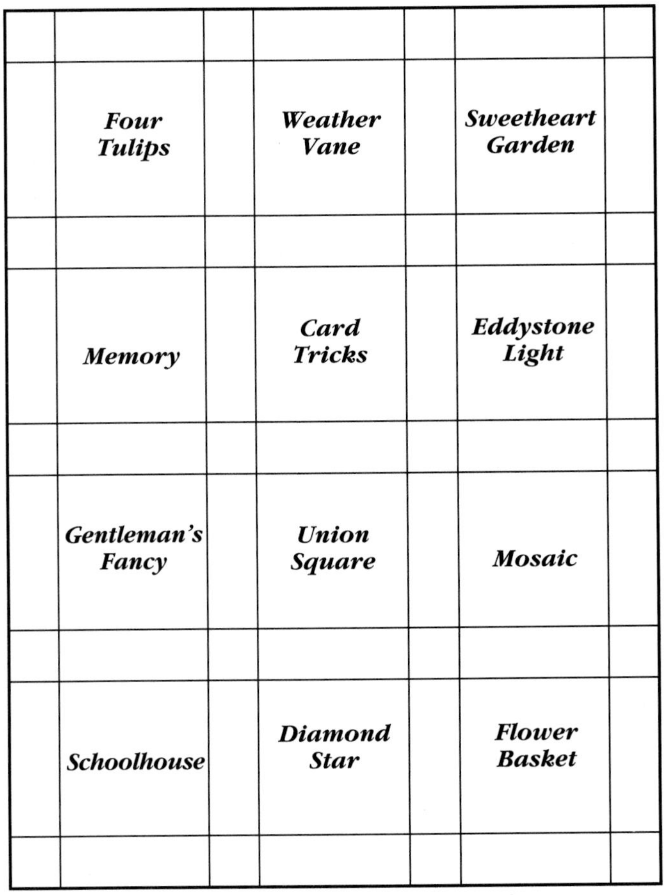

Four Tulips	*Weather Vane*	*Sweetheart Garden*
Memory	*Card Tricks*	*Eddystone Light*
Gentleman's Fancy	*Union Square*	*Mosaic*
Schoolhouse	*Diamond Star*	*Flower Basket*

Finished Size:
Quilt: 52" x 68"
Blocks: 12 (12") Sampler Blocks

Fabrics:
Red print	⅓ yard
Lt. red print	¼ yard
Coral print	¼ yard
Green print	⅓ yard
Dk. blue print	¼ yard
Black print	¼ yard
Lt. yellow print	¼ yard
Gold print	⅝ yard
Beige print	¼ yard
Muslin	1 yard
Dk. brown print	½ yard
Med. brown print	1½ yards
Med. brown print (for binding)	½ yard
Backing	4⅛ yards

1 package of ¼" green double-fold bias tape

Note: If you prefer to make your own bias strips for stems, refer to Bias Strips for Stems, page 146.

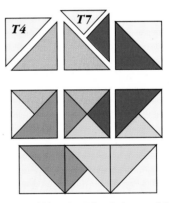

Card Tricks Block Assembly

Card Tricks

Pieces to Cut

T4	4 muslin
	2 beige print
	2 green print
	2 gold print
	2 coral print
T7	4 muslin
	2 beige print
	2 green print
	2 gold print
	2 coral print

Instructions
Assemble pieces as shown in Block Assembly diagram.

9

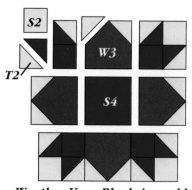

Weather Vane Block Assembly

Union Square Block Assembly

Gentleman's Fancy Block Assembly

Weather Vane

Pieces to Cut
S2	4 lt. yellow print
	4 red print
S4	1 red print
T2	16 lt. yellow print
	8 red print
W3	4 dk. blue print

Instructions
Assemble pieces as shown in Block Assembly diagram.

Union Square

Pieces to Cut
S2	4 muslin
S4	1 dk. brown print
T2	16 red print
	8 muslin
T4	4 lt. red print
T7	4 muslin
	4 lt. yellow print

Instructions
Assemble pieces as shown in Block Assembly diagram.

Gentleman's Fancy

Pieces to Cut
S4	1 gold print
T4	4 muslin
	4 black print
T7	8 coral print
	4 black print
	4 green print

Instructions
Assemble pieces as shown in Block Assembly diagram.

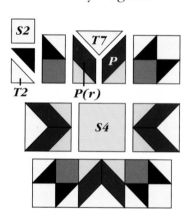

Memory Block Assembly

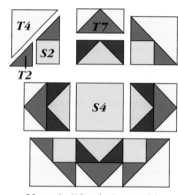

Mosaic Block Assembly

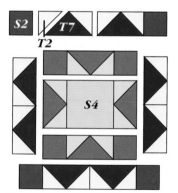

Eddystone Light Block Assembly

Memory

Pieces to Cut
S2	4 muslin
	4 lt. red print
S4	1 lt. yellow print
T2	8 muslin
	8 black print
	8 gold print
T7	4 muslin
P	4 dk. brown print
P(r)	4 dk. brown print

Instructions
Assemble pieces as shown in Block Assembly diagram.

Mosaic

Pieces to Cut
S2	4 lt. yellow print
S4	1 lt. yellow print
T2	8 muslin
	8 green print
	8 dk. blue print
T4	4 muslin
T7	4 green print
	4 gold print

Instructions
Assemble pieces as shown in Block Assembly diagram.

Eddystone Light

Pieces to Cut
S2	4 med. brown print
	4 coral print
S4	1 gold print
T2	16 muslin
	8 lt. yellow print
T7	8 red print
	4 coral print

Instructions
Assemble pieces as shown in Block Assembly diagram.

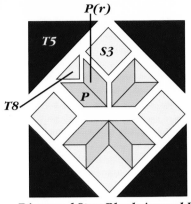

Diamond Star Block Assembly

Instructions
1. Assemble pieces as shown in Block Assembly diagram.
2. Embellish as desired with a button for doorknob and flowers made from yo-yos. (Referring to instructions on page 145 and making 1¾" circle template from pattern on page 157, make 2 yo-yos.) Add stems and leaves with embroidery stitches on page 145.

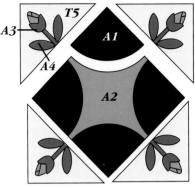

Sweetheart Garden Block Assembly

Diamond Star

Pieces to Cut
S3	4 muslin
T5	4 dk. brown print
T8	4 muslin
P	4 gold print
P(r)	4 gold print

Instructions
Assemble pieces as shown in Block Assembly diagram.

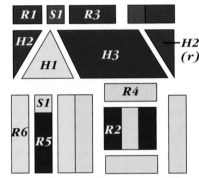

Schoolhouse Block Assembly

Schoolhouse

Pieces to Cut
S1	2 med. brown print
	1 lt. yellow print
R1	2 dk. blue print
R2	2 dk. brown print
	1 gold print
R3	1 dk. blue print
R4	2 gold print
R5	1 dk. brown print
R6	2 lt. yellow print
	2 gold print
H1	1 lt. yellow print
H2	1 dk. blue print
H2(r)	1 dk. blue print
H3	1 red print

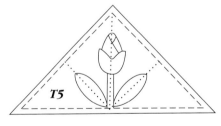

Four Tulips Block Assembly

Four Tulips

Pieces to Cut
12½" square	1 muslin

4 (8") strips of ¼" green double-fold bias tape (or refer to page 146 to make stems from bias strips)

Instructions
1. Referring to Freezer Paper Hand Appliqué, page 143, prepare pieces for appliqué : 4 (C1) green, 4 (C2) coral, 4 (C3) gold.
2. Fold muslin square in quarters to locate center. Lightly trace appliqué design on ¼ muslin square. Repeat on remaining quarters until entire design is traced.
3. Appliqué pieces in the following order: stems, C1, C2, and C3, as shown in Block Assembly diagram.

Sweetheart Garden

Pieces to Cut
A1	4 black print
A2	1 coral print
A3	4 green print
A4	8 green print
T5	4 muslin
3½" circles	4 coral print

4 (2") strips of ¼" green double-fold bias tape (or see page 146 to make stems from bias strips)

Instructions
1. Fold T5 triangle in half and finger-press to mark center. Fold sides of triangle to center as shown in Diagram A and finger-press to mark leaf placement lines. Pin 2" strip of bias tape from raw edge of base of triangle along center line. Appliqué. Repeat for remaining triangles.

Diagram A: Appliqué Placement

2. Referring to Freezer Paper Hand Appliqué, page 143, use template A3 and A4 to prepare 4 calyxes and 8 leaves. Appliqué leaves in place as shown.

Referring to Fabric Rosebuds, page 146, use 3½" circles to make 4 rosebuds. Position top of rosebud 1⅜" above top of each stem and pin. Position calyx, checking to be sure that it will cover both top of stem and bottom of rose-bud. Adjust placement if necessary. Appliqué rosebud and then calyx on each triangle.

3. Assemble pieces as shown in Block Assembly diagram.

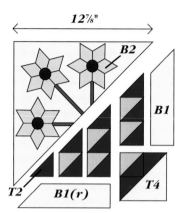

Flower Basket Block Assembly

Flower Basket

Pieces to Cut
12⅞" square   1 muslin
Note: Cut muslin square in half diagonally. Set aside 1 triangle. Cut smaller muslin pieces from remaining triangle.

B1	1 muslin
B1 (r)	1 muslin
T2	12 red print
	6 beige print
T4	1 muslin
B2	18 gold print

3 scraps of dk. brown print (for yo-yos)
1 (4") strip of ¼" green double-fold bias tape
2 (2½") strips of ¼" green double-fold bias tape (or refer to page 146 to make stems from bias strips)

Instructions
1. Trace corner dots on all B2 pieces. To make 1 flower: With right sides facing and raw edges aligned, join 2 (B2) pieces, stitching from corner dot to corner dot. Add another B2 to make 3-piece unit as shown in Diagram B, Figure 1. Press and trim seams as shown. Make a second unit in same manner. With right sides facing, raw edges aligned, and

Diagram B: Piecing Flowers
Figure 1

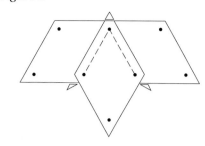

Figure 2

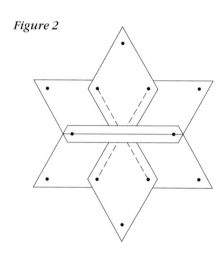

Figure 3

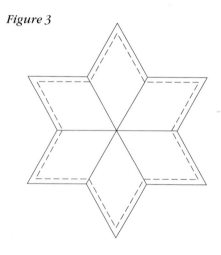

stitching from corner dot to corner dot, join 2 units. (See Figure 2.)

2. Make 2 more flowers. Turn under all outside seam allowances and hand-baste. (See Figure 3.)

3. Fold large muslin triangle in half and finger-press to mark center. Beginning at raw edge of triangle base, pin 4" strip of bias tape along center fold line. Referring to Flower Basket Block Assembly diagram, position

center flower, overlapping top of stem ¼". Appliqué center flower and stem.

Position 2 side flowers and pin. Tuck 2½" strips of bias tape ¼" under flowers and extend strips to raw edge of muslin triangle. Appliqué stems and flowers. Remove basting stitches.

Referring to Yo-Yos, page 145 and making 1¾" circle template from pattern on page 157, make 3 yo-yos and appliqué to flower centers.

4. Referring to Block Assembly diagram, piece bottom basket unit of block. Join top and bottom units of block as shown.

Golden Star Sashing

Pieces to Cut
S4	6 gold print
	14 dk. brown print
T2	48 gold print
W1	7 med. brown
W2	10 med. brown
4½" x 12½" strips	14 med. brown

Instructions
1. Assemble 7 center sashing units as shown in Diagram C, Figure 1, and 10 side sashing units as shown in Figure 2.

Diagram C: Piecing Sashing
Figure 1

Figure 2

2. Referring to Diagram D and photograph, assemble horizontal rows as shown. Join horizontal rows to complete quilt top.

Quilting

Quilt in-the-ditch around all pieces, blocks, and sashing. Trace Pumpkin Seed quilting pattern for center squares in Weather Vane, Sweetheart Garden, Memory, Eddystone Light, Gentleman's Fancy, Union Square, and Mosaic blocks. Referring to photograph, quilt Card Tricks and Diamond Star blocks as shown, spacing lines of quilting 1⅜" apart. Trace Diamond Square quilting pattern in outer setting squares and centers of inner sashing strips.

Binding

Refer to Binding, page 150.

Diagram D:
Quilt Top Assembly

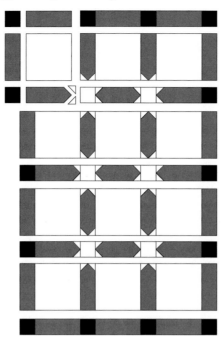

BAZAAR TIP
Get organized! These words are the bazaar planner's motto. Electing a general chairperson is the first step, but individual committees are equally important. You will want committees for each bazaar booth, as well as for publicity, decorations, and set-up. Chairpersons should gather volunteers, discuss assignments, and agree on a schedule so that your bazaar's goals can be reached on time.

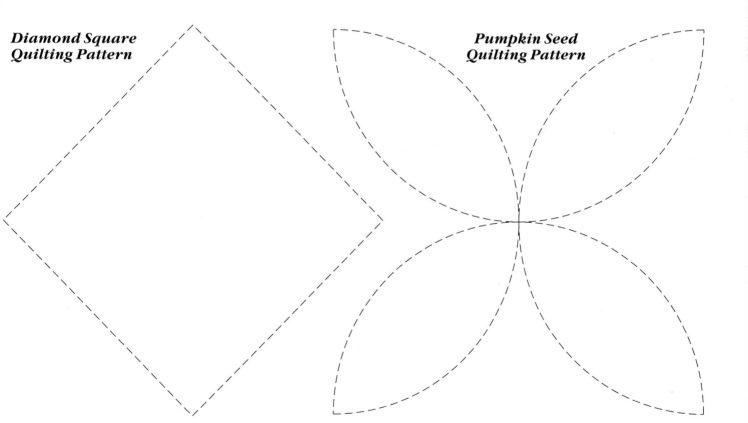

Diamond Square
Quilting Pattern

Pumpkin Seed
Quilting Pattern

Patchwork Pillows

Above: Easy Patchwork Pillows
Far right: Pillow with Flanged Border
Left: Patchwork Pillow with Ruffle and
Mock Double Ruffle Pillow

14

Using blocks from the *Star Harvest Sampler* quilt, you can make a batch of decorative patchwork pillows that will provide plenty of variety for your bazaar's pillow booth. By adding borders to the basic blocks, using the measurements below, you can also make pillows in two sizes. All these pillows are made with "envelope backs" that make them fast to assemble and easy to remove for washing or for changing pillow covers to suit the season.

Three pretty ways to add finishing touches to patchwork pillows are from Judy Cantwell of Birmingham, Alabama. Judy, a popular teacher at a local quilt shop, has devised her own method for making graceful ruffled pillows, including a version that looks as if it has a double ruffle. Another favorite is the elegant pillow with a flanged border that is surprisingly fast and easy to make.

Easy Patchwork Pillow

Fabrics and Materials
12½" pieced block
Border and envelope back   ½ yard
Muslin (optional)
Thin batting (optional)
Thread to match fabrics
14" or 16" pillow form

Pieces to cut

	14" Pillow	16" Pillow
Border	2 (1¾" x 12½")	2 (2¾" x 12½")
	2 (1¾" x 15")	2 (2¾" x 17")
Envelope back	2 (12" x 15")	2 (12" x 17")

Instructions
1. With right sides facing and raw edges aligned, join short border strips to opposite sides of pieced block. Press seams toward borders. Join long border strips to remaining sides. Press.
Note: Pillow front may be quilted, if desired, before assembling pillow cover. Layer muslin, batting, and pillow top (right side up). Pin-baste. Quilt by hand or machine.
2. To make envelope back: On 1 long edge of 1 rectangle, turn under ¼" and then ⅝". Press. Topstitch ½" from folded edge and then edgestitch. Repeat for second rectangle.

    With wrong side up, smooth 1 rectangle on table. Referring to Diagram A, overlap second rectangle (wrong side up) so that 2 pieces form a square that is same size as pillow top. Machine-baste overlapped edges. Pin envelope opening closed.

Diagram A: Envelope Back

Basting line   Basting line

Overlap

3. With right sides facing, raw edges aligned, and using a ½" seam, stitch envelope back to pillow front, stitching completely around square. Unpin envelope opening. Clip corners and turn through envelope opening. Insert pillow form.

Patchwork Pillow with Ruffle

Fabrics and Materials
12½" pieced block
Border and envelope back   ½ yard
Print for ruffle   1 yard
Thread to match fabrics
Pearl cotton
14" or 16" pillow form

Instructions
1. Referring to Easy Patchwork Pillow for dimensions, cut borders and envelope backs for either 14" or 16" pillow. Cut strips to make ruffle as follows: For 14" pillow, cut 4 (7" x 44") strips. For 16" pillow, cut 4 (7" x 44") strips and 1 (7" x 22") strip.
2. Referring to Easy Patchwork Pillow, Steps 1 and 2, join borders to pieced block and make envelope back.
3. To make ruffle: With right sides facing, join ends of strips to form continuous strip. With wrong sides facing and raw edges aligned, fold strip in half lengthwise and press. Divide strip into 4 equal sections, marking each division with a pin.

    Working each of the 4 sections separately, position 50" length of pearl cotton about ⅜" from raw edge of ruffle, leaving about 3" on each end. Holding pearl cotton in place as you sew, zigzag over pearl cotton, using widest and longest stitch setting. (Be careful not to catch pearl cotton in zigzag stitching.)

    Find center of each side of pillow front and mark with a pin. Referring to Diagram B, with right sides facing, position end of 1 section of ruffle at 1 center point on pillow front and pin. Wrap ends of zigzag-gathering threads and pearl cotton firmly around pin. Hold other end of pearl cotton and gather ruffle, distributing fullness as evenly as possible. Aligning raw edges, pin gathered section to pillow front, allowing extra fullness in corners. Repeat for remaining sections.

Diagram B: Ruffled Pillow

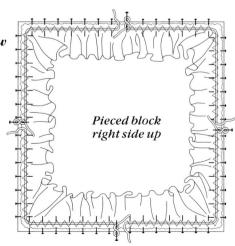

Pieced block right side up

4. With right sides facing, raw edges aligned, and ruffle sandwiched between, stitch envelope back to pillow front, using a ⅝" seam. *Hint: At each corner, instead of pivoting to change direction sharply, round the corners slightly. This will prevent corners from looking "pinched."* Clip corners and turn through envelope opening. Insert pillow form.

Mock Double Ruffle Pillow

Fabrics and Materials
12½" pieced block	
Border and envelope back	½ yard
Print for inner ruffle	½ yard
Contrasting print for outer ruffle	¾ yard
Threads to match fabrics	
Pearl cotton	
14" or 16" pillow form	

Instructions
1. Referring to Easy Patchwork Pillow for dimensions, cut borders and envelope backs for 14" or 16" pillow. Cut strips for mock double ruffle as follows: For 14" pillow. From inner ruffle print, cut 4 (2¾" x 44") strips; from outer ruffle print, cut 4 (4¾" x 44") strips.

For 16" pillow: From inner ruffle print, cut 4 (2¾" x 44") strips and 1 (2¾" x 22") strip; from outer ruffle print, cut 4 (4¾" x 44") strips and 1 (4¾" x 22") strip.
2. Referring to Easy Patchwork Pillow, Steps 1 and 2, join borders to pieced block and make envelope back.
3. With right sides facing and raw edges aligned, join 1 inner ruffle strip to 1 outer ruffle strip along 1 long edge. Repeat for remaining strips. Join ends of strips to form a continuous strip. With wrong sides facing and raw edges aligned, fold strip in half lengthwise and press, forming mock double ruffle strip as shown in Diagram C.

Diagram C: Mock Double Ruffle Strip

Fold

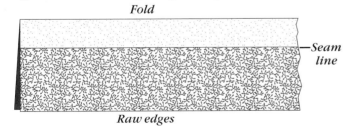

—*Seam line*

Raw edges

4. Referring to Patchwork Pillow with Ruffle, Steps 3 and 4, complete pillow.
Note: When gathering and attaching ruffle, be sure to place seamed side of pieced ruffle face down.

Pillow with Flanged Border

Fabrics and Materials
12½" pieced block	
Borders	⅛ yard
Envelope back and flanged borders	⅝ yard
Thread to match fabrics	
14" or 16" pillow form	

Pieces to Cut
	14" Pillow	16" Pillow
Border	2 (1½" x 12½")	2 (2½" x 12½")
	2 (1½" x 14½")	2 (2½" x 16½")
Flanged border	2 (2¾" x 14½")	2 (2¾" x 16½")
	2 (2¾" x 19")	2 (2¾" x 21")
Envelope back	2 (12" x 19")	2 (13" x 21")

Instructions
1. Referring to Easy Patchwork Pillow, Step 1, join borders to pieced block. Join flanged borders to block in same manner.
2. Referring to Easy Patchwork Pillow, Step 2, make 19"-square envelope back for 14" pillow or 21"-square envelope back for 16" pillow. To reinforce part of back that extends behind flange, use thread to match envelope back and topstitch over previous stitching, 3" from each edge. (See Diagram D.)

Diagram D: Back for Flanged Pillow

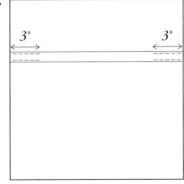

3"   3"

3. With right sides facing and raw edges aligned, stitch pillow front to envelope back, using ½" seam. Clip corners, turn, and press.
4. On pillow front, topstitch in-the-ditch between border and flanged borders through all layers.
5. Insert pillow form.

Cupboard
Collection

You'll find lots of timesaving techniques in these projects for the kitchen and home. Fusible appliqué makes quick work of the fragrant Happy Home Spice Mat. Machine-quilting the Evening Star Pot Holder is fast and easy when you follow the nonstop quilting diagram. You can dress up kitchen towels in a jiffy with lace doilies. And the Blue Jean Mug Tote, shining with an Evening Star block, makes wise use of fabric scraps.

Machine-Quilted Pot Holders

Get off to a quick start with three patchwork pot holders that update traditional block patterns with today's best shortcuts. Border strips frame the blocks, so there's no binding to add. Best of all, each design has its own nonstop machine-quilting diagram. If you've been thinking that it's time you gave quilting on the sewing machine a try, you'll never find a better first project!

You'll want to make several sets, using different prints for border strips and lots of pretty scraps.

Fabrics and Materials (for 3 pot holders)

Patterns, pages 152 and 154	
Dk. print	¼ yard
Assorted scraps of lt., med., and dk. prints	
Thick batting	
Silver silicone-coated ironing board cover fabric	¼ yard
⅜"-wide grosgrain ribbon	½ yard

Pieces to Cut (for 3 pot holders)

1½" x 6½" strip	6 dk. print
1½" x 8½" strip	6 dk. print
8½" square	3 batting
	3 ironing board cover fabric
6" piece	3 grosgrain ribbon

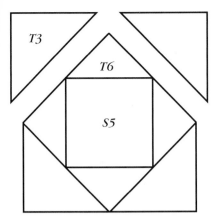

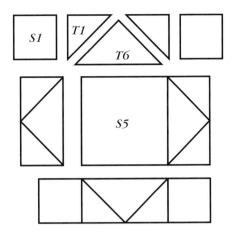

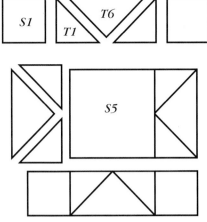

**Diamond-in-a-Square
Block Assembly**

Mosaic Variation Block Assembly

Evening Star Block Assembly

Pieces to Cut for Diamond-in-a-Square Block
Template S5	1 dk. print
Template T3	4 med. print
Template T6	4 lt. print

Pieces to Cut for Mosaic Variation Block
Template S1	4 med. print
Template S5	1 med. print
Template T1	8 lt. print
Template T6	4 dk. print

Pieces to Cut for Evening Star Block
Template S1	4 lt. print
Template S5	1 med. print
Template T1	8 dk. print
Template T6	4 lt. print

Instructions
1. Piece 3 blocks as shown in Block Assembly diagrams. Press blocks.
2. With right sides facing and raw edges aligned, pin 1½" x 6½" strips to 2 opposite sides of each block. Machine-stitch and press seams toward borders. Add 1½" x 8½" strips to remaining sides of each block in same manner. Press seams toward borders.
3. To assemble each pot holder: For hanger loop, fold 6" ribbon in half. With raw edges aligned, place loop on right side of pieced block at 1 corner. Baste ribbon ends at corner.

Stack batting square, pieced block (right side up), and ironing board cover fabric (right side down). Stitch, leaving an opening for turning and catching ends of hanger loop in seam. Clip corners, turn, and press. Slipstitch opening closed.

Make 2 more pot holders in same manner.
4. To machine-quilt each pot holder, refer to Machine Quilting, page 150, and Nonstop Quilting diagram below for each block.
Note: For Evening Star, before beginning to quilt, refer to Evening Star Nonstop Quilting diagram and lightly mark lines of machine quilting that will cross S5 (center) square.

Place machine needle in fabric exactly at X (starting point) and stitch in-the-ditch following arrows as shown in diagram. At corner, with machine needle down, raise presser foot and pivot pot holder. Lower presser foot and continue stitching.

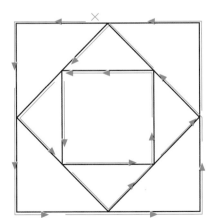

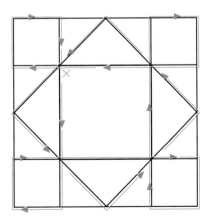

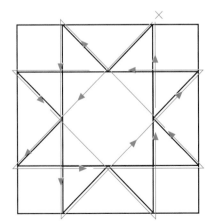

**Diamond-in-a-Square
Nonstop Quilting**
Start at X and follow arrows.

Mosaic Variation Nonstop Quilting
Start at X and follow arrows.

Evening Star Nonstop Quilting
*Start at X and follow arrows.
After returning to X, continue stitching
completely around border.*

Teatime Table Set

Place mats and napkins are bazaar staples, but they go beyond basic when they're all dressed up for tea. Donna Gallagher, of Westerville, Ohio, creates a lovely tea party setting with soft prints and fabric flowers blossoming on place mats, napkins, and a ruffled tea cozy. Her methods are fast and easy, using fused appliqué and a new quick-turn technique that eliminates binding the edges of the place mats.

Place Mats

Fabrics and Materials (for 4 place mats)
Patterns, page 24

Cream print	⅞ yard
Muslin	⅞ yard

Scraps of green prints, blue prints
Thin batting
Paper-backed fusible web

Pieces to cut

14" x 18" rectangle	4 cream print
14" x 19" rectangle	4 muslin
14" x 19" rectangle	4 batting

Instructions

1. With right sides facing, fold 1 cream print rectangle into quarters, aligning raw edges. Pin. To cut off corners, starting at raw-edge corner, mark 3½" from corner on 2 adjacent sides. Lay a ruler across corner and draw a line from point to point. Cut on marked line through all layers. Remove pins and unfold.

2. *Note:* Here is a new method for making an opening for turning. With right sides facing, fold 1 muslin backing rectangle in half widthwise. (See Diagram.) Starting at 1 outside raw edge and using a ½" seam along fold, stitch for 5"; stop and backstitch. Clip threads. Leave 4" unstitched in center for opening, backstitch, and then continue stitching to other outside raw edge. Trim fold, leaving ¼" seam allowance. Press seam open.

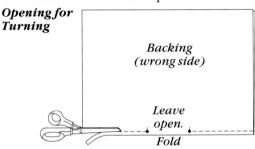

Opening for Turning

Backing (wrong side)

Leave open.

Fold

3. Layer muslin rectangle (right side up) and cream octagon (right side down) and stitch completely around, using ¼" seam and following edge of octagon. Do not turn.

4. Smooth batting on flat surface and lay place mat on top with cream octagon facing batting. Stitch again along same stitching line. Trim corners, excess fabric, and batting. Turn through opening in back of place mat. Slipstitch opening closed. Press.

5. Topstitch around place mat ¼" from outside edge. Lightly mark a line 2" in from this stitching line and topstitch. *Hint: Start and stop topstitching in the corner where the yo-yo will be attached. Flower and leaves will cover the thread ends.*

6. Repeat steps 1-5 to make 3 more place mats.

7. To make yo-yo flower: Refer to Yo-Yos, page 145, making 3½" circle template from pattern on page 157. Trace 4 circles on right side of blue print fabric. After making each yo-yo, leave a 6" tail of thread attached in center.

To make leaves: Referring to Paper-backed Fusible Web, page 143, trace 12 leaves on paper side of web. Fuse to wrong side of green print fabrics following manufacturer's instructions. Cut out leaves. Remove paper, and referring to photo for placement, fuse 3 leaves to each place mat.

Machine-appliqué, if desired. Using tail of thread in center of yo-yo, tack 1 flower to center of leaves.

Napkins

Fabrics and Materials (for 4 napkins)
Blue print   1¾ yards
Scraps of green prints, blue prints
Paper-backed fusible web

Pieces to Cut
15" square   8 blue print

Note: Two different coordinating prints may be used for napkin fronts and backs, if you prefer. You will need ⅞ yard of each fabric.

Instructions
1. With right sides facing and raw edges aligned, stitch squares together, leaving a small opening along 1 edge for turning. Turn and press. Slipstitch opening closed. Topstitch, if desired. Make 3 more napkins.

2. Referring to Place Mats, Step 7, add 2 leaves and 1 yo-yo flower to each napkin as shown in photo.

Tea Cozy

Fabrics and Materials
Patterns, page 24

Cream print	½ yard
Muslin	½ yard
Dk. floral print	¼ yard

Scraps of blue prints, green prints, floral prints
Paper-backed fusible web
Assorted buttons
Thin batting
14" (¼"-wide) satin ribbon

Pieces to Cut

13" x 15" rectangle	2 cream print
	2 muslin
	2 batting
3½" x 45" strip	2 dk. floral print

Instructions
1. Enlarge gridded cozy pattern. Trace pattern on cream print and muslin rectangles and cut out.

2. Trace basket triangle pattern 8 times on paper side of fusible web. Following manufacturer's instructions, fuse web to wrong side of blue print and cut out. To make basket, position triangles on right side of cozy front, referring to photo for placement and aligning bottom row of triangles 1½" from bottom edge of cozy. Fuse.

3. Trace leaf pattern 7 times on paper side of fusible web. Fuse web to wrong side of green print fabrics and cut out leaves. Remove paper and set leaves aside.

4. Referring to Place Mats, Step 7, and using floral prints, make 4 yo-yos. Set aside.

5. For pansies, cut 7 (7" x 3½") rectangles from assorted floral print fabrics. With right sides facing, fold rectangles widthwise and pin. Trace pansy pattern on 1 side. Stitch along traced line. Trim fabric ¼" outside stitching line. Cut a small slit in center of 1 side and turn. Repeat to make 6 more.

To make a pansy: Lay 1 pansy petal with slit side down on flat surface for base. Fold 1 petal loosely into thirds and tack center of folded petal to top of

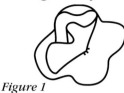
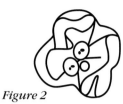
base. (See Diagram, Figure 1.) Add another petal in same manner. Stitch 2 or 3 buttons in center of pansy. (See Figure 2.) Make a second pansy in same manner.

To make a bud: Fold remaining petal in thirds and stitch 1 button on top of folds.

6. Referring to photo, position leaves, pansies, and yo-yo flowers on cozy front. Set flowers aside and fuse leaves in place.

7. To make ruffle: With right sides facing, join dark floral print strips to make 1 long strip. On each end, turn raw edge under ¼", machine-stitch, and press. With *wrong* sides facing and raw edges aligned, fold strip in half lengthwise and press. Run a gathering thread along long raw edge of strip. Gather ruffle to fit cozy front.

8. Smooth 1 batting rectangle on flat surface and place cozy front on top, right side up. Pin together. Trim excess batting. Repeat for cozy back.

9. Beginning and ending ½" from bottom of cozy front and with raw edges aligned, pin ruffle to right side of cozy front. Cut 4" piece of ribbon and fold in half to make a loop. With raw edges aligned, pin loop on ruffle at center top. Stitch ruffle to cozy front through all layers, catching ends of loop in seam.

10. With right sides facing, raw edges aligned, and ruffle sandwiched between, stitch cozy front to back. Turn.

11. With raw edges aligned, stitch muslin lining pieces together, leaving 4" open at center top. Do not turn. With right sides facing, slip cozy inside lining, matching side seams. Stitch together along straight bottom edges. Turn through opening in lining. Slipstitch opening closed and press.

12. Position flowers on cozy front and tack in place through all layers. Make a bow from remaining ribbon and tack to front of cozy on basket.

BAZAAR TIP

Make sets in different colors, or with two place mats instead of four, so that your customers will have plenty of choices.

Create a small display featuring a place mat, napkin, and tea cozy with lovely china, tea accessories, and romantic flowers. It won't take much space, but it will definitely attract attention.

Basket, Leaf, and Pansy patterns are full-size.

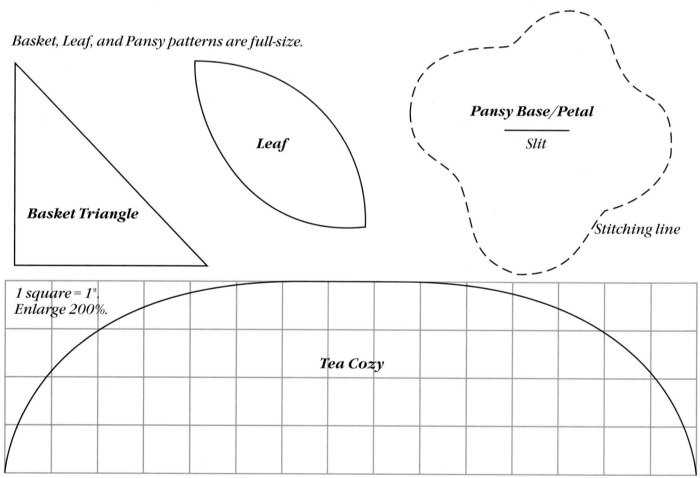

Basket Triangle

Leaf

Pansy Base/Petal

Slit

Stitching line

1 square = 1".
Enlarge 200%.

Tea Cozy

Extend 9".

Tulip Table Runner

This small table runner is blooming with springtime tulips, quickly applied with fused appliqué. The "on point" piecing looks tricky, but the only trick is how easy it is to do. The colorful border needs no binding, and the straight-line design makes machine quilting a breeze.

Fabrics and Materials

Patterns, page 27	
Cream print	¼ yard
Lt. blue print	¼ yard
Blue floral print	¾ yard
Med. blue print	⅛ yard
Small scrap of yellow print	
Thread to match fabrics	
Thin batting	
Paper-backed fusible web	

Pieces to Cut *

Template T9	8 lt. blue print
Template T10	6 cream print
20" x 32" rectangle	1 blue floral print
	1 batting
2¼" x 45" strips	3 blue floral print

▶▶▶ TIME-SAVER

*Using a rotary cutter, you can quick-cut triangles without using the patterns! From light blue print, cut 4 (5½") squares. Cut squares in half diagonally to yield 8 (T9) triangles.

From cream print, cut 2 (10¼") squares. Cut the squares into quarters diagonally to yield 8 (T10) triangles. (You'll need 6 (T10s) for the Table Runner. Save the extra triangles for another project.)

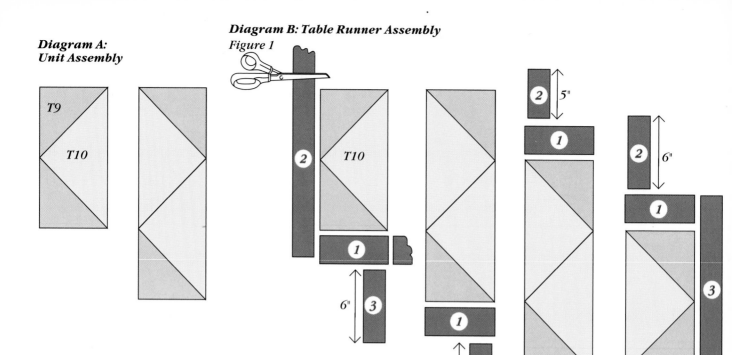

Diagram A:
Unit Assembly

Diagram B: Table Runner Assembly
Figure 1

T9

T10

T10

2

1

3

6"

5"

2

1

5"

2

1

3

1

2

1

5"

6"

2

1

3

6"

Unit A

Unit B

Unit C

Unit D

Figure 2

4

4

Instructions

1. Referring to Diagram A, assemble T9 and T10 triangles in units as shown. Make 2 of each unit.

2. Referring to Diagram B, Figure 1, follow sequence of numerals shown in red for joining 2¼"-wide blue floral border strips to units. With right sides facing and raw edges aligned, join strip #1 to bottom of Unit A. Trim strip as shown. Press seam toward strip.

With right sides facing and raw edges aligned, add strip #2, stitching along entire length of pieced rectangle plus just-added border strip. Trim as shown.

Cut remainder of this strip into 2 (5") strips and 2 (6") strips. Now join remaining border strips, except strip #4, to all units as shown, trimming as necessary and adding just cut 5" and 6" strips.

3. With right sides facing and raw edges aligned, join units. (See Figure 2.) Press seams open. Trim excess border fabric.

Add strips #4 to top and bottom as shown, trimming as necessary. (Save remainder of strip for another bazaar project.) Press seams toward border strips.

4. To make tulip appliqués: Referring to Paper-backed Fusible Web, page 143, trace 16 leaves, 8 stems, and 8 buds on paper side of fusible web. Following manufacturer's instructions, fuse leaves and stems to wrong side of medium blue print and cut out. Fuse buds to wrong side of yellow scrap and cut out. Remove paper backing. Referring to photograph for placement, position pieces on T9s in this order: buds, stems, leaves. Fuse in place.

5. To make opening for turning: With right sides facing, fold 20" x 32" blue floral print rectangle in half widthwise. Referring to Teatime Place Mat, Step 2, page 23, make opening in backing. Press seam open and press backing flat.

6. Layer backing (right side up) and top (right side down) and pin. Stitch completely around edges of table runner top.

Smooth batting on table and place table runner (top side down) on top. Pin. Stitch again along same stitching line.

Trim excess batting and backing, clip corners, and turn through opening in backing. Slipstitch opening closed and press.

7. Referring to Machine-Quilting, page 150, machine-quilt in-the-ditch around center rectangle and inside border.

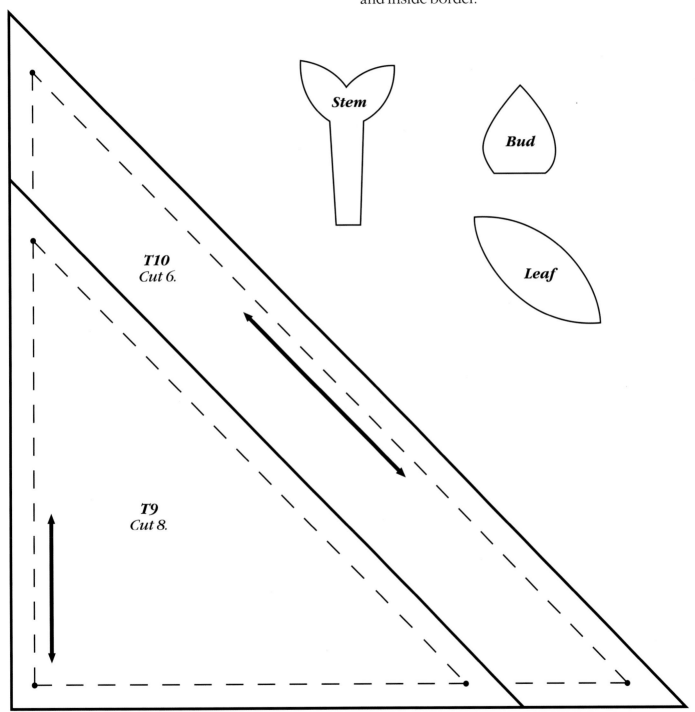

Stem

Bud

Leaf

T10
Cut 6.

T9
Cut 8.

Lacy Heart Dish Towel

Fabrics and Materials
Pattern, page 156
17" x 27" dish towel
6" square lace doily
Small scrap of print fabric
Thread to match fabric

Instructions
1. Referring to Freezer Paper Hand Appliqué, page 143, and using Heart #1 pattern on page 156, appliqué heart to center of doily as shown in photo.
2. Center doily on point 3" from bottom edge of dish towel and pin. Slipstitch finished edges of doily to towel.

Quick Lace Dish Towel

Fabrics and Materials
17" x 27" dish towel
9" round lace doily

Instructions
1. Cut doily in half. Center 1 doily half on 1 end of dish towel, with cut edge of doily just above stitching line of hem. Pin. (Set aside other half of doily for another towel or pot holder.)
2. Slipstitch finished edge of doily to towel.
3. Turn hemmed edge of towel up over straight edge of doily. Slipstitch hem in place. Press.

Quick Lace Pot Holder

Fabrics and Materials
8" square purchased pot holder
9" round lace doily
12" (¼"-wide) red grosgrain ribbon
1 large red satin rosette with leaves

Instructions
1. Remove binding stitches from bottom half (on point) of pot holder opposite hanger loop to expose raw edge of pot holder.
2. Fold doily in quarters; press. Cut doily into quarters along pressed fold lines.
3. Aligning raw edges of 1 doily quarter and pot holder, slipstitch finished edge of doily in place, leaving binding free. (Set aside remaining quarters for other pot holders.)
4. Replace binding over edges of pot holder. Using matching thread, machine-stitch binding in place.
5. Tie ribbon in a bow and tack to doily, sewing through top layer only. (See photo.) Tack rosette to knot of bow.

Quick Lace Kitchen Set

Turning ready-made items into designer creations is certainly the fastest way to make bazaar projects. These kitchen accessories designed by Eileen Westfall, of Edmonds, Washington, are pretty, lightning-fast, and have the touch of handwork that will make them a real hit with your customers.

Stenciled Hot Mats

Inexpensive sisal rug squares, which are sold at import stores, inspired Cecily Zerega, of Fairfield, Connecticut. Combining her love for traditional patchwork designs and the pleasure of stenciling, she created these great-looking mats for the counter or table.

Fabrics and Materials
Patterns, pages 158 and 159
Basic stenciling supplies listed on page 143
12" sisal rug squares
Tracing paper
Acrylic stencil paint
Repositionable spray stencil adhesive (optional)
Clear acrylic spray varnish (optional)

Instructions
1. Select 1 of the stencil designs on pages 158-159. Trace entire pattern on tracing paper. (See small sketch on pattern page to produce entire design.) Check fit on sisal square. Adjust pattern if needed.
2. Referring to Stenciling, page 143, mark and cut stencils, making a separate stencil for each color.
3. Using masking tape, tape sisal square to work surface. Spray stencil with adhesive or use masking tape to firmly adhere stencil to sisal square. Using a stencil brush, apply stencil paint. (Because of the porous fibers, you will need to apply a thick coat of paint.)
4. Allow to dry several hours. Stencil second color if applicable. Spray with varnish if desired.

Easy Aprons

Bright calico hearts and patchwork pockets turn plain purchased aprons into bazaar best sellers. The apron pocket design can also be made into a pretty mat that releases a spicy aroma whenever a hot pot is placed on it. And tiny gingham aprons with playtime pot holders are great for three to six year-old girls who just love to "help" in the kitchen.

There's also a special barbecue apron designed for those who never want to be "out of pocket." It has pockets to hold a cordless phone, a pencil, and a notebook. The pattern given is for a man's apron, but we all know that the executive chef may be Mom. You may substitute any basic apron pattern as long as there's room for the sturdy pleated pockets.

Happy Home Apron

Fabrics and Materials
White or solid bib apron
Muslin .... ¼ yard
Scraps of lt. prints, dk. prints
Thin batting
Paper-backed fusible web

Pieces to Cut
6½" square	2 lt. print
8½" square	2 muslin
	2 batting
1½" x 6½" strip	4 dk. print
1½" x 8½" strip	4 dk. print

Instructions
1. To make pockets: Make templates using House pattern, page 157. Referring to Paper-backed Fusible Web, page 143, turn templates over and trace 2 reversed designs on paper side of fusible web. Following manufacturer's instructions, fuse design to wrong side of dark print scraps and cut out. Remove paper backing and fuse 1 house to center of each 6½" light print square.

With right sides facing and raw edges aligned, join 1 (1½" x 6½") strip to top and bottom of each block. Press seams toward borders. Add 1½" x 8½" strips to remaining sides of each block. Press seams toward borders.

For each pocket, stack batting, pieced block, (right side up), and muslin square. Stitch, leaving an opening at bottom for turning. Clip corners, turn, fold in raw edges ¼", and press.

2. Position pockets on apron and pin. Using thread to match border, first topstitch ¼" from edge and then edgestitch around sides and bottom of each pocket.

3. Using Heart #1, #2, and #3 patterns on page 156, trace 3 hearts on paper side of fusible web. Following manufacturer's instructions, fuse to wrong side of dark print scraps and cut out. Remove paper backing. Position on apron bib as desired and fuse.

★ BAZAAR TIP
Since you don't spend your time sewing the aprons, you'll have time to decorate them in different styles and color schemes for your bazaar. Select other designs for the fused appliqués from the patterns on page 156, in addition to the hearts shown here. For instance, because the pockets are the same size as the Machine-Quilted Pot Holders on page 20, you can make some pockets from those designs as well, using thin batting and omitting the hanger loop.

Happy Home Spice Mat

Fabrics and Materials (for 1 spice mat)
Muslin .... ¼ yard
Scraps of lt. prints, dk. prints
Thick batting
Paper-backed fusible web
Spicy potpourri

Pieces to Cut
8½" square	1 batting
6½" square	1 lt. print
1½" x 6½" strip	2 dk. print
1½" x 8½" strip	2 dk. print
7" x 8½" rectangle	2 muslin
3½" x 7" rectangle	1 muslin

Instructions
1. Refer to Happy Home Apron, Step 1, to piece 1 (8½") block.
2. To make envelope-style back: On 1 long side of each 7" x 8½" muslin rectangle, turn under ¼" twice and press. Stitch hem. Repeat for other rectangle. With wrong side up, place 1 rectangle on table. Place second rectangle (wrong side up) on top of first, so that they form 8½" square and hemmed edges overlap at center. Machine-baste raw edges where rectangles overlap.
3. Stack batting, pieced block (right side up), and back (right side down). Stitch completely around square. Remove basting in back. Turn through opening.
4. Make a bag for potpourri by folding 3½" x 7" rectangle in half widthwise to measure 3½" square. Stitch sides, leaving an opening. Fill bag loosely with potpourri and stitch opening closed.
5. Insert muslin bag inside spice mat through opening.

Little Chef Apron

Fabrics and Materials
Gingham .... ½ yard
Scrap of red fabric
Scrap of batting
6" piece of red worsted-weight yarn
Pointed yarn needle

Pieces to Cut
3½" x 44" strip	1 gingham
10½" x 17" rectangle	1 gingham
4½" square	2 gingham
	1 batting

Instructions
1. To make waistband sash: Fold 3½" x 44" strip in half widthwise to locate center. Measure 5" on each side of center and mark on each long edge of

strip. Beginning at 1 end of strip and ending at mark, turn under ¼" twice on 1 long edge and press. Repeat on other end of strip. Machine-stitch, backstitching at mark. Repeat for remaining long edge of strip, leaving center 10" unhemmed. Turn both unhemmed center edges under ½" and press.

2. With right sides facing and hemmed edges aligned, fold strip in half lengthwise and stitch ends. Referring to Diagram, turn and flatten strip to make point. Press.

Folding Pointed Ends

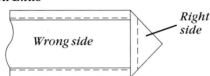

3. To hem sides and bottom of apron: Turn under ¼" twice on each end of 10½" x 17" rectangle and press. Machine-stitch hem. On bottom edge, turn under ¼" and then 1". Press. Machine-stitch hem.

4. Run gathering threads ½" and ¼" from top raw edge of apron. Pull threads to gather to 8".

5. With wrong sides facing, fold waistband in half lengthwise. Insert apron between folded edges of waistband and stitch through all layers.

6. To make pot holder: Stack batting square, 1 (4½") gingham square (right side up), and 1 square (right side down). Stitch, leaving an opening for turning. Turn, fold under raw edges, and edgestitch around entire pot holder.

7. Trace Heart #1, page 156, on right side of red fabric. Cut out on marked line and pin to center of pot holder. Referring to Machine Appliqué, page 143, appliqué heart to pot holder.

8. To make hanger loop, thread yarn needle with yarn and stitch through 1 corner of pot holder. Knot ends of yarn together.

Executive Chef Apron

Fabrics and Materials
60"-wide pin-striped denim   1 yard
Scrap of red fabric
Threads to match fabrics
Paper-backed fusible web
Scrap of fusible interfacing

Note: If 60"-wide pin-striped denim is not available, use 1⅝ yards of 45"-wide pin-striped denim. Stripes on apron and pocket should run lengthwise. If solid denim is used, pocket can be cut on crosswise grain, requiring only 1 yard of 45"-wide denim.

Pieces to Cut

9" x 19" rectangle	1 denim
2¼" x 28¾" strip	2 denim
2¼" x 20¼" strip	1 denim
3" x 5" rectangle	1 fusible interfacing
	1 paper-backed fusible web

Instructions

1. Enlarge and transfer apron pattern to fabric and cut out, adding ⅜" seam allowance. Zigzag or serge raw edges to prevent fraying. Turn ⅜" to wrong side on all edges of apron body except bottom. Press.

2. For waist tie, press under ⅜" on both long edges and 1 end of 1 (2¼" x 28¾") strip. Trim corners. With wrong sides facing and edges aligned, fold strip in half lengthwise and press. Edgestitch. Make other tie in same manner.

For neck loop, finish long edges of 2¼" x 20¼" strip in same manner.

3. On wrong side of apron, align raw ends of neck loop with raw edges at corners of bib top; pin. In same manner, align raw ends of waist ties with raw edges at corners of apron body; pin.

To hem edges of apron: Beginning at 1 corner of bottom edge and continuing around top of apron to opposite corner, topstitch ¼" from edge, catching waist ties and neck loop in stitching. For stability, edgestitch at waist ties and neck loop.

For hem, turn under 1" on bottom of apron and topstitch.

4. To make pocket: On 9" x 19" rectangle, turn under ⅜" on 1 long edge and both ends. Press. Turn under ⅝" hem at top edge, press, and topstitch.

Measure and mark vertical lines as shown in Pocket Diagram, Figure 1.

To make phone pocket: Referring to Figure 2 and beginning at left edge of pocket, fold along line #1 to align with left edge of pocket, forming ½" pleat. Pin at bottom hem and press. Fold along line #2 to meet line #3, forming second pleat. Pin and press. Center pocket on apron body, with bottom of pocket 6⅝" from bottom of apron. Pin securely. Topstitch to apron along each side of line #5.

Unpin pleats and topstitch on each side of lines #3 and #4 to make pencil pocket. Edgestitch left edge of phone pocket to apron, folding pleat out of the way. Re-fold pleats and pin to apron. Beginning at top right corner of pocket rectangle, edgestitch right side and bottom of pocket, catching pleats in seam. Edgestitch bottom again for stability.

5. Following manufacturer's instructions, fuse 3" x 5" interfacing rectangle to wrong side of red fabric scrap. Trace bow tie pattern on paper side of fusible web. Fuse to interfacing/red fabric piece. Cut out pattern on marked line. Remove paper backing. Center bow tie on apron bib, 1½" from top. Machine-appliqué in place.

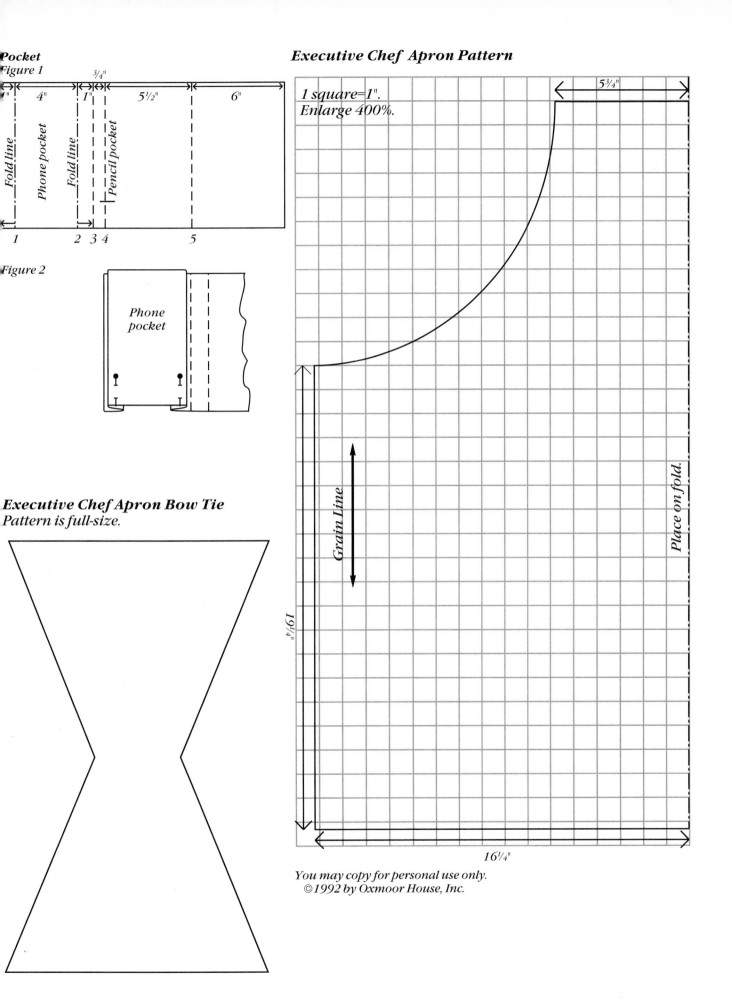

Pocket
Figure 1

1"   4"   1"   ¾"   5½"   6"

Fold line
Phone pocket
Fold line
Pencil pocket

1   2 3 4   5

Figure 2

Phone pocket

Executive Chef Apron Bow Tie
Pattern is full-size.

Executive Chef Apron Pattern

1 square=1".
Enlarge 400%.

5¾"

Grain Line

Place on fold.

19¼"

16¼"

You may copy for personal use only.
©1992 by Oxmoor House, Inc.

33

Easy Totes and Lunch Bag

A plain tote bag becomes a special bazaar item when you add a big patchwork pocket or a colorful stencil design. And the Apple-A-Day Lunch Bag is an easy, reusable alternative to a throw-away paper bag.

Patch Pocket Tote

Fabrics and Materials
Patterns, page 152
Solid canvas	½ yard
Scraps of assorted lt., med., and dk. prints	
Muslin	⅓ yard
Thin batting	

Pieces to Cut
Template S2	4 med. background print
Template S4	1 med. or dk. print
Template T2	8 lt. print
Template T7	4 med. background print
2" x 8½" strip	2 dk. print
2" x 11½" strip	2 dk. print
11½" square	1 muslin
	1 batting
18" square	2 canvas
2½" x 18" strip	2 canvas

Instructions
1. Referring to Diagram A, piece block. With right sides facing and raw edges aligned, join 2" x 8½" strips to top and bottom of pieced block. Press seams toward borders. Add 1 (2" x 11½") strip to each remaining side in same manner. Stack batting, pieced block (right side up), and muslin. Stitch, leaving an opening at bottom for turning. Clip corners, turn, fold raw edges in ¼", and press. If desired, referring to Evening Star Nonstop Quilting diagram, page 21, machine-quilt block.
2. To make pocket: Center block on right side of 1 canvas square, with top of block 3½" from top of canvas. Topstitch ⅜" and then ⅛" from edge around sides and bottom of block, catching folded edges in stitching.
3. To assemble tote bag: With right sides facing and raw edges aligned, stitch squares together around

sides and bottom. Zigzag seams to reinforce and finish edges. Do not turn.
4. To form box bottom of bag: Align bottom seam and 1 side seam to form a triangle as shown in Diagram B. Pin bottom and side seams together 2½" away from point of triangle. Repeat to form triangle on other side of bag bottom. Flatten bottom and stitch straight across base of triangle, removing pin just before needle reaches it. Trim off triangles and reinforce trimmed seams with zigzag stitching.

Diagram A: Block Assembly

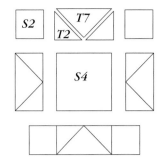

Diagram B: Tote Bag Bottom

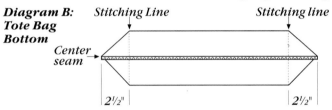

5. To make handles: Fold 1 (2½" x 18") strip into thirds lengthwise and press. Turn long raw edge under ¼" and topstitch closed. Repeat to make another handle.
6. At top of bag, turn raw edge under ¼" and then 1½". Press. With handle seam facing up, insert raw ends of 1 handle under top hem, 4½" from each side seam. Edgestitch along lower edge of folded hem, catching handles in seam. Turn bag right side out. Raise handle into carrying position. Edgestitch around top of bag, catching handles in seam. Repeat for second handle on bag back.
7. To shape bag at corners: With bag right side out, flatten bottom of bag. Starting at 1 bottom corner and going straight up to top of bag, make a fold parallel to side seam. (See Diagram C.) Pin along fold. Topstitch ¼" away from folded edge from top to bottom. Repeat to shape 3 more corners.

Diagram C: Shaping corners

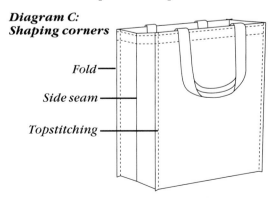

▶▶▶ **TIME-SAVER**

You can add the patchwork pocket, made in Step 1 on the previous page, to a plain purchased tote bag. Make several bags using lots of scraps in different color combinations.

Stenciled Tote

Fabrics and Materials

Plain solid tote bag, at least 13" wide
12" x 13" cardboard
Basic stenciling supplies listed on page 143

Instructions

Select 1 of the stencil designs on pages 158-159. Referring to Stenciling, page 143, prepare stencil. Insert cardboard inside tote bag and stencil design. Let dry.

Apple-A-Day Lunch Bag

Fabrics and Materials

Denim or canvas   ⅜ yard
Scraps of red print, green print
Paper-backed fusible web
1 Velcro dot (optional)

Pieces to Cut

11½" x 13" rectangle   2 denim or canvas

Instructions

1. Using Apple #1 and small leaf pattern, page 156, trace 1 apple and 1 leaf on paper side of fusible web. Following manufacturer's instructions, fuse apple and leaf to wrong sides of red scrap and green scraps. Using pinking shears, cut fabric ¼" outside paper shapes. Remove paper backing.

Center apple horizontally on right side of 1 rectangle, 3½" from 1 end. Position leaf. Following manufacturer's instructions, fuse in place. Topstitch ¼" inside pinked edges of apple and leaf.
2. With right sides facing and raw edges aligned, stitch bag front to back around sides and bottom.
3. To form box bottom: Referring to Patch Pocket Tote, Step 4, align bottom and side seams. Pin seams together 2" away from points of triangle. Complete bottom as before. Turn bag right side out. Turn top raw edge under ¼" twice, press and topstitch.
4. To shape lunch bag: Referring to Patch Pocket Tote, Step 7, make folds at corners of bag. Press. Do not stitch.

At top of bag, hold front and back corner folds together. Fold down 1". Press. Fold down again 1" and press. Add Velcro dot to fasten bag if desired.

Blue Jeans Tote Bags

It seems that everyone is joining in the effort to save our environment. Your bazaar can help by recycling worn denim jeans into attractive alternatives to disposable products. Designers Susan Rand and Paula Kemperman of Wild Goose Chase, Grand Rapids, Michigan, suggest using the mug tote to carry your personal mug to meetings or to work, eliminating the need for throw-away cups. And the Pine Tree Grocery Tote will solve the "paper-or-plastic" dilemma!

Evening Star Mug Tote

Fabrics and Materials
Patterns, page 39
Worn adult blue jeans, washed and pressed
Assorted scraps for Evening Star block
24" shoelace
Paper-backed fusible web

Pieces to Cut
Template A   8 dk. print
Template B   4 background print
Template C   4 background print
Template D   1 med. print
9"-long cylinder of blue jean leg

Instructions
1. Referring to Diagram, piece Evening Star block. Trim away ¼" seam allowance on all sides so that block size is 4". Following manufacturer's instructions, fuse webbing to wrong side of pieced block. Remove paper backing.

Center Evening Star block between seams on blue jeans leg cylinder, with top of block 2⅜" from top edge of denim. Fuse block in place. With thread that matches denim, machine-appliqué block to denim.

Evening Star Block Assembly

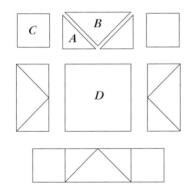

2. Turn leg inside out. Stitch across bottom. Zigzag raw edge of seam to prevent fraying.
3. Zigzag raw top edge. Fold 1" to wrong side and stitch to form a casing.
4. Turn tote right side out. Cut ½" slit in outside layer of casing only. Thread shoelace through casing for drawstring. Knot ends of drawstring together.

BAZAAR TIP
Why not sell mugs along with the Mug Totes? These sets will make attractive gifts that express concern for the environment. In exchange for good publicity, a local business could support your effort by donating the mugs or by selling them to you at a wholesale price.

Pine Tree Grocery Tote

Fabrics and Materials
Patterns, page 39
Striped denim or canvas*   1¼ yards
Print   ⅔ yard
Worn adult blue jeans, washed and pressed
Thin batting
Assorted lt. and dk. scraps
Paper-backed fusible web (optional)

Pieces to Cut
Template A   1 dk. print
                            4 lt. print
Template B   1 lt. print
     B(r)   1 lt. print
Template C   3 dk. print
Template D   1 med. print
20" x 44" rectangle*   1 denim or canvas
                            1 print (for lining)
                            1 batting

Note: If you prefer, ⅔ yard solid denim or canvas may be used for outer bag instead of striped fabric. If striped fabric is used, rectangle should be cut so that stripes run lengthwise.

Instructions
1. Referring to Diagram A, make 1 Pine Tree block. For hand appliqué, press seam allowance under so that finished square measures 8". Set aside.

Diagram A

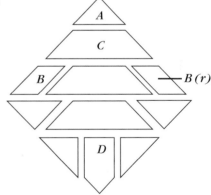

▶▶▶ TIME-SAVER
Instead of doing hand appliqué, plan to machine-appliqué the Pine Tree block to the bag. Trim the seam allowance so that the block measures 8". Following the manufacturer's instructions, fuse webbing to the wrong side of the pieced block. Remove the paper backing and set the block aside.

2. For bottom of bag, open 1 seam of 1 upper leg of blue jeans and press flat. With remaining leg seam centered vertically, cut 11½" x 20" rectangle. Turn under ¼" seam allowance on each 20" edge and press.

Diagram B

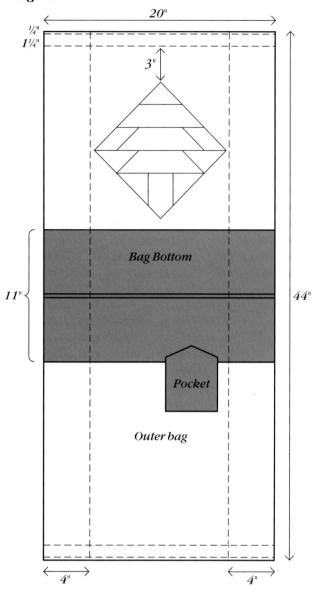

For body of bag, referring to Diagram B, center bag bottom right side up on right side of 20" x 44" outer bag fabric. Topstitch long edges of bag bottom in place.

If desired, remove 1 back patch pocket from jeans, cutting through jeans at outside edge of pocket without cutting into pocket stitching. Turn pocket over and trim away fabric under pocket. Position pocket as shown in diagram and topstitch it in place.

3. Referring to Diagram B, mark right side of outer bag fabric with vertical fold lines 4" from each long edge. Mark horizontal lines ¼" and 1¼" from top and bottom edges.

Stack print lining (right side down), batting, and outer bag (right side up). Pin layers securely. Machine-baste along all marked lines with thread that matches outer bag fabric. Basting will not be removed.

4. Referring to Diagram B, mark 3" down from 1¼" basting line for Pine Tree block placement. Center block on point as shown. Using thread to match outer bag, hand-appliqué block in place. (To machine-appliqué, fuse block in place. Machine-appliqué around edge of block through all layers.) If desired, hand or machine-quilt in-the-ditch and ¼" from outer edge of block.

5. With right sides facing and raw edges aligned, fold bag in half and stitch side seams. Machine-zigzag seams to reinforce and finish edges. Do not turn.

6. To form box bottom: Referring to Patch Pocket Tote, Step 4, page 35, align bottom and side seams. Pin seams together 3½" away from points of triangle. Complete bottom as before.

7. Turn bag right side out. To hem top of bag: Turn under top edge at ¼" basting line. Press. Turn under again at 1¼" basting line. Topstitch hem.

8. On right side of bag front, fold along 1 vertical basting line and topstitch ⅛" from fold, from top to bottom corners. Repeat for remaining 3 sides.

9. For handles, cut waistband from jeans (at least 24"-long), trimming close to seamed edge. Cut waistband in half. (If you prefer, 1"-wide nylon webbing may be used instead.) Finish ends of strips with zigzag stitching or by folding under raw edge. Pin ends of 1 strip to inside hem of bag front, 3" from each topstitched side. Repeat for bag back. Topstitch ends of strips securely to bag.

BAZAAR TIP

A group of volunteers working together to make bazaar projects can accomplish wonders. You can share ideas, shortcuts, and encourage each other. Getting together for regularly scheduled work sessions allows your group to use assembly-line methods for greatest efficiency. Advance planning and coordination is a must for real success. A workshop leader should make sure that there are plenty of supplies on hand. All of the fabric should be washed and ironed so that it's ready to be cut.

If it's difficult for your group to get together for work sessions, it's still a good idea to meet frequently. Regular meetings let members "show-and-tell" about what they've been working on. Seeing what others are making can provide new ideas and inspirations, and help to keep your group motivated and on schedule.

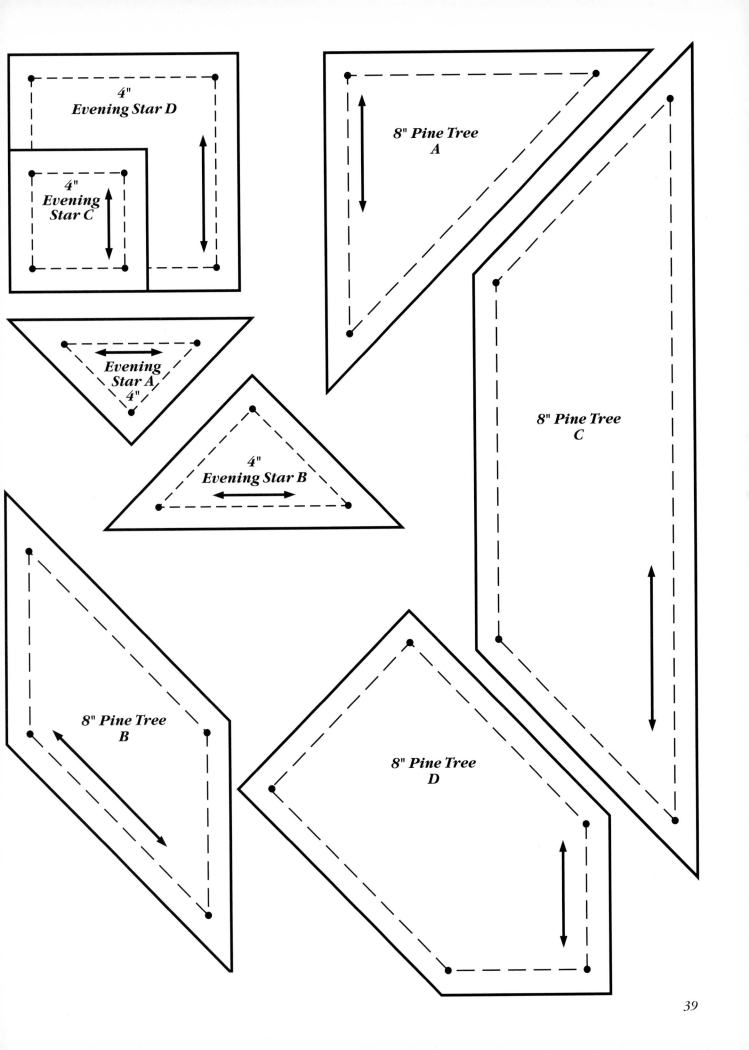

4"
Evening Star D

4"
Evening Star C

8" *Pine Tree*
A

Evening Star A
4"

4"
Evening Star B

8" *Pine Tree*
C

8" *Pine Tree*
B

8" *Pine Tree*
D

Happy Patchwork

Six tiny characters made from one basic pattern emerge from the pockets of a Storyteller Apron, made of inexpensive ticking. The Schoolhouse block in bright colors becomes a caddy for crayons and drawing paper. A Patchwork Cat, easy Fabric Necklaces, and a mischievous Siamese Cat Belt are sure to delight little girls. And you'll find many more ideas for wonderful projects that children (and their parents) will love.

Art Caddy & Patchwork Cat

Clear, bright colors make the School-house block an inviting home for crayons, scissors, coloring books, and drawing paper. It's also a safe place for bringing treasured drawings home from school. When the schoolhouse is closed with its Velcro tab, it's a colorful addition to the decor of a child's room.

The charming patchwork cat delights both children and adults with its primitive "scrappy" style. Soft and washable, it will make a lovable toy or a warm decorative accent for a country-style home.

Schoolhouse Art Caddy

Fabrics and Materials
Patterns, pages 152–154

Blue pindot	⅜ yard
Red print	¼ yard
Yellow print	¼ yard
Green	⅛ yard

Scraps of yellow, purple fabrics
Scrap of 1"-wide eyelet lace
1 (½") white button
1 (1") square of Velcro
12½" x 26" rectangle of thin batting
2 (12½") squares of corrugated cardboard

Pieces to Cut

Template S1	2 red print
	1 green
Template R1	2 blue pindot
Template R2	2 yellow print
	1 purple
Template R3	1 blue pindot
Template R4	2 purple
Template R5	1 red print
Template R6	2 green
	2 purple
Template H1	1 solid yellow
Template H2	1 blue pindot
Template H2 (r)	1 blue pindot
Template H3	1 red print
8" x 26" rectangle	1 red print
12½" square	1 blue pindot
12½" x 26" rectangle	1 blue pindot
1¾" x 12½" strip	1 yellow print
1½" x 12½" strip	2 yellow print
1½" x 28" strip	2 yellow print
1¾" x 26" strip	1 green
4" x 6" rectangle	1 green

Instructions

1. Referring to Schoolhouse Block Assembly diagram on page 11, piece block. Stitch on button for doorknob, and slipstitch eyelet lace to windows for curtains.

2. To make front panel: With right sides facing and raw edges aligned, join 1 long edge of 1¾" x 12½" yellow print strip to left edge of Schoolhouse block. Join 12" square blue pindot to remaining long side of yellow print strip.

To make closure tab: With right sides facing, fold 4" x 6" green rectangle in half widthwise. Stitch long edge and 1 end, leaving 1 end open. Turn, center seam on back, and press. With right sides facing and raw edges aligned, pin open end to right edge of pieced block, beginning at lower edge of roof. At other end, stitch hook side of Velcro to wrong side of strip.

With right sides facing and raw edges aligned, join 1½" x 12½" yellow print strips to each end of assembled panel. Press. Join 1½" x 28" yellow print strips to top and bottom of panel.

3. To make pocket: With right sides facing and raw edges aligned, stitch 26"-long green strip to red print rectangle along 1 long edge. Press seam toward green strip. To bind top edge of pocket: Press long raw edge of green strip under ¼". Fold green strip in half lengthwise and slipstitch to wrong side of pocket at seam line.

4. Place 12½" x 26" blue pindot lining (right side up) on table. Aligning raw edges at sides and bottom, lay pocket (right side up) on lining. Hand or machine-baste together.

5. To assemble: Smooth front panel (right side down) and batting on flat surface. Lay 1 cardboard square on each end of rectangle. Place lining/pocket (right side up) on top. For self-binding, fold yellow print strips over edges of batting and cardboard to lining/pocket. Turn under ¼" and pin. Slipstitch binding in place, mitering corners.

6. Make small running stitches through all layers along center of spine between cardboard squares. Fold green closing tab around caddy and position loop side of Velcro on back. Handstitch Velcro to secure.

Patchwork Cat

Fabrics and Materials
Patterns, pages 46 and 152

Muslin	¼ yard
Scraps of assorted print fabrics	
9" x 10½" print for backing	
¼"-wide ribbon	½ yard
Polyester stuffing	

Pieces to Cut

Template T1*	42 muslin
	42 prints

▶▶▶ **TIME-SAVER**

*Instead of tracing templates, you can quick-cut triangles from squares using a rotary cutter. Cut 21 (2⅜") squares from muslin and 21 (2⅜") squares from prints. Then cut the squares in half diagonally to yield 42 muslin triangles and 42 print triangles.

Of course, to make the fastest Patchwork Cat, you can use pre-printed patchwork fabric. Cut the fabric to measure 9" x 10½" and begin the assembly instructions with Step 2.

Instructions

1. With right sides facing and raw edges aligned, stitch together long edges of 1 muslin and 1 print triangle. Press seam toward print. Join remaining triangles to form 42 squares. Join squares to make pieced rectangle 6 squares across by 7 squares down, as shown in Diagram.

2. Referring to Diagram, position Patchwork Cat pattern on *right* side of patchwork fabric. Trace and cut out. (Be careful not to ravel seams of patchwork.) Trace pattern on *wrong* side of backing print and cut out.

Pattern Placement

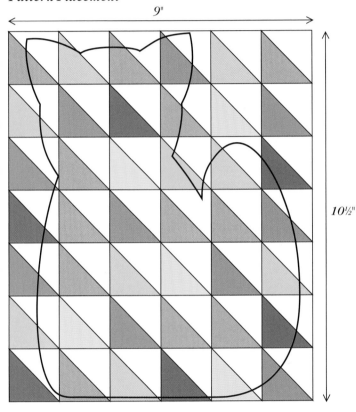

3. With right sides facing and raw edges aligned, stitch patchwork front to backing, leaving an opening for turning. Clip curves and clip angle at tail, stopping just short of stitching line. Turn and stuff firmly. Slipstitch opening closed.
4. Tie ribbon around neck. Tack through knot to secure.

BAZAAR TIP

Some bazaars simply say "Moms and Dads only, please." But for the many bazaars that welcome children, fun features can be planned so that children will feel like special guests.

Offer a children's craft workshop. For a small fee, provide some basic supplies: washable paint, scraps of fabric, lace, and ribbon, sponges cut for sponge painting, rubber stamps, etc. (Many of these craft supplies can be gathered by asking for donations.) You will need volunteers to help, and many ideas for projects. All projects should be planned so that children can have fun, use lots of creativity, and be proud of the finished product.

Have a "dress up" room. Old prom dresses, out-of-date tuxedos, and other donated clothing can be very entertaining for children. With some hats, scarves, sashes, and jewelry, they'll have great fun creating costumes. This room definitely needs to have a mirror—an unbreakable one, of course.

Invite a storyteller, a clown, or a magician to entertain your young visitors. Or, using the Storyteller Apron, page 48, let children take turns making up stories themselves. Another activity that encourages children to entertain each other is a paper bag puppet show. Children can create their own hand puppet characters by decorating small paper bags with paint, crayons, felt, or yarn.

Set up a special "Children's Bazaar" selling small items that children can buy, such as penny candy or toys. If your bazaar is held during the holidays, the Children's Bazaar can give youngsters the chance to do their own secret gift shopping. Sell inexpensive items like bookmarks, sachets, kitchen magnets, or small decorated picture frames. Using donated materials, volunteers can help children gift wrap their own secret gift purchases.

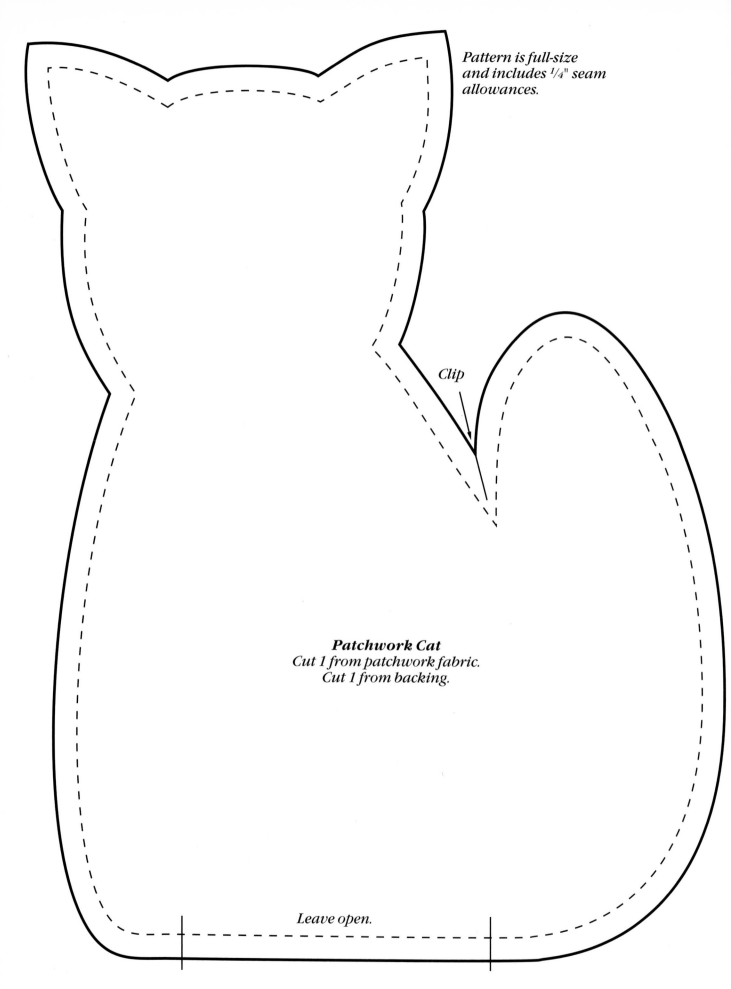

Pattern is full-size and includes ¹/₄" seam allowances.

Clip

Patchwork Cat
Cut 1 from patchwork fabric.
Cut 1 from backing.

Leave open.

Ragged Bow Vest

Fabrics and Materials
Child's cotton vest (lined)
Scraps of assorted solid fabrics
125 (³⁄₁₆") multi-colored wooden beads
Large quilting pins
Rotary cutter, cutting mat, and ruler
Thread to match vest lining

Pieces to Cut
1" x 3" strip   250 solid fabric

Instructions
1. With right sides of both strips facing up, place 2 strips together. Vary color combinations. Pin strips on vest to determine best color arrangement.
2. Using thread that matches vest lining, insert threaded needle through right side of vest beneath point at which center of bow will be. (Knot will be concealed by bow.) Center bead on 1 pair of fabric strips. Handstitch bead through all layers, securing and gathering fabric strips beneath bead in 1 motion. Repeat for remaining strips.

Ragged Bow Comb

Fabrics and Materials (for 1 comb)
3" plastic ornamental hair comb
Scraps of assorted fabrics
2 small satin roses with stems
Rotary cutter, cutting mat, and ruler

Pieces to Cut
½" x 6" strips   26 solid fabric

Instructions
1. Cut V-shaped notch in both ends of each strip.
2. Insert pairs of strips between teeth of comb. Tie each pair in double knot at top of comb.
3. Insert stems of both roses between teeth in center of comb and around top. Twist stems together to secure roses.

Pretty Bows for Girls

Bows, bows, and more bows in delicious colors cover this little girls' vest like candy sprinkles. Use your favorite pattern to make a simple lined vest and dress it up with bows of fabric scraps and wooden beads. The unfinished edges of cotton fabric give the bows just the right "ragged" look. You'll need two strips for each of 125 bows to cover a size-six vest. Use a rotary cutter to cut those strips, and you'll finish the job in record time. The pretty matching combs are even quicker to make.

Storyteller Apron
Carol Tipton

48

Storyteller Apron

The child who dons this Storyteller Apron spins tales of make-believe adventures, and the tiny figures tucked inside the pockets are the cast of characters. A group of children can pass the apron so that everyone has a turn as the storyteller, or the characters can come out on their own for group play. Making up stories with the Storyteller Apron can also be a great back-seat activity on long car trips.

Carol Tipton, of Calera, Alabama, designed this wonderful project which delighted her daughter, Sarah. Carol remembered an apron her mother made for her when she was Sarah's age. Simply cut from sturdy ticking, it takes a pretty shape when the neckline is gathered with grosgrain ribbon.

Fabrics and Materials
Patterns, pages 50 and 51
Apron:
Blue-and-white striped ticking   1 yard
1 package of ½"-wide yellow rickrack
1 package of ⅝"-wide blue rickrack
1 package of ¼"-wide red double-fold bias tape
⅝"-wide red grosgrain ribbon   2 yards
Characters:
Pig: fabric scraps of pink (body), blue (bib); blue
    embroidery floss, 1 (⁵⁄₁₆") 2-hole white button
Bunny: fabric scrap of white (body); 8" (¼"-wide)
    pink ribbon; tan, pink embroidery floss
Cat: fabric scraps of black (body), yellow (dress);
    white, green embroidery floss
Girl: fabric scraps of white (body), green (dress); red
    ribbon scrap; black, yellow embroidery floss
Boy: fabric scraps of red print (shirt), brown (body),
    blue (pants); white, black embroidery floss
Bear: fabric scraps of yellow print (pants), brown
    (body); scrap of red double-fold bias tape, tan
    embroidery floss
Polyester stuffing
Dressmaker's carbon
Thread to match fabrics

To Make Apron:
1. Enlarge and transfer pattern for apron and pocket to ticking and cut out. Using dressmaker's carbon, mark outlines for armholes on apron, and cut out.
2. Turn under ½" along top edge of pocket and press. Lay blue rickrack on wrong side of pocket with scallops extending above pocket edge. Topstitch ⅛" from folded edge.
3. On both ends of pocket, turn under ½" and press. With right sides up, position pocket on apron, matching bottom edges and aligning stripes. Topstitch pocket sides ⅛" from folded edges. Topstitch line in center of pocket from top to bottom.
4. Measure 3½" down from top edge of pocket and draw a horizontal line across pocket. Lay yellow rickrack along this line, turning raw edges under ¼" at each end. Topstitch along center of rickrack through all layers.
5. Using double-fold bias tape, bind side and bottom edges of apron and arm openings.
6. On top edge of apron, fold 2" to wrong side to form a casing and press. On right side of apron, topstitch blue rickrack 1¾" from fold at top of apron. Thread grosgrain ribbon through casing. Pull ribbon to gather neckline. Tie ribbon ends in a bow at back of apron.

To Make Characters:
1. To make body for pig, bunny, cat, and girl: Cut body fabric into 2 (5½") squares. Trace pattern on wrong side of 1 square of body fabric. Transfer facial features to right side of body.

With right sides facing, pin second body square to first. Stitch along traced line. Trim seam allowances to ⅛". Make 1" vertical slit through back layer only. Clip curves and between legs and turn body through slit. Stuff. Whipstitch slit closed.

To make body for boy and bear: Cut 1 (3" x 10") rectangle from brown fabric and 1 (3" x 10") rectangle from pants fabric. With right sides facing and raw edges aligned, join brown fabric to pants fabric along 1 long edge. Press seam toward pants fabric. Cut this piece in half to make 2 (2½" x 5") rectangles.

Place body pattern on wrong side of pieced rectangle with waistline of pattern at seam line of rectangle. Referring to instructions above, make body for boy and bear.
2. For each animal, trace pattern for ears twice onto wrong side of 1 layer of body fabric. With right sides facing, pin second layer to first and stitch along traced lines, leaving bottom edges open for turning. Trim seams to ⅛". Clip corners and turn. Turn under ⅛" seam allowances along opening and slipstitch ears to body.

Pig: Fold tips of ears to front and tack. Sew on button for nose.

Bear: Trace 1 muzzle onto body fabric and cut out, adding ⅛" seam allowance. Turn under seam allowance, add small amount of stuffing, and appliqué to bear's face.

3. Referring to Facial Pattern for placement and photo for colors, embroider facial details using 2 strands of embroidery floss. (See Embroidery Stitches, page 145.) Use French knots for eyes and running stitches for other details.

4. To make clothing for characters:

Pig: Trace bib pattern onto fabric and cut out, adding ⅛" seam allowance. Fold seam allowance to wrong side of bib and handstitch all around. Gather top straight edge to ¾". Tack gathered edge to neck of pig.

Girl, Cat, and Boy: Trace dress/shirt pattern onto wrong side of 1 layer of fabric. With right sides facing, pin second layer to first. Stitch shoulders and sides along marked lines, leaving neck, arms, and hem open. Trim seam allowances to ⅛". Clip curves and turn. Turn under ⅛" hems at all openings and handstitch.

Bear: To make suspenders, fold bias tape in half to form a V. Tack fold of V to center back at waistline. Fold loose ends over shoulders and tack each end with French knot at front waistline.

5. To finish characters:

Girl: Braid 15 (4½") strands of yellow floss. Tie each end of braid with floss. Tack braid across top of head along seam line. Tack ribbon scrap to side of head for bow.

Boy: Take 1 stitch with 2 strands of black embroidery floss from front to back at top of head. Clip thread, leaving about 1" tail on each side. Tie tails in double knot. Trim ends to ¼". Make 8 knots as shown in pattern.

★ BAZAAR TIP

The six characters in the pockets of the Storyteller Apron offer a wide range of possibilities for make-believe adventures. But, taking a tip from the major toy companies, offer the characters separately as well, so that children can select the ones that have special appeal for them. Make a range of characters with different body colors, hair colors, and clothing. Discount the price for a complete set with the apron and six characters, and set the price for individual characters a little higher.

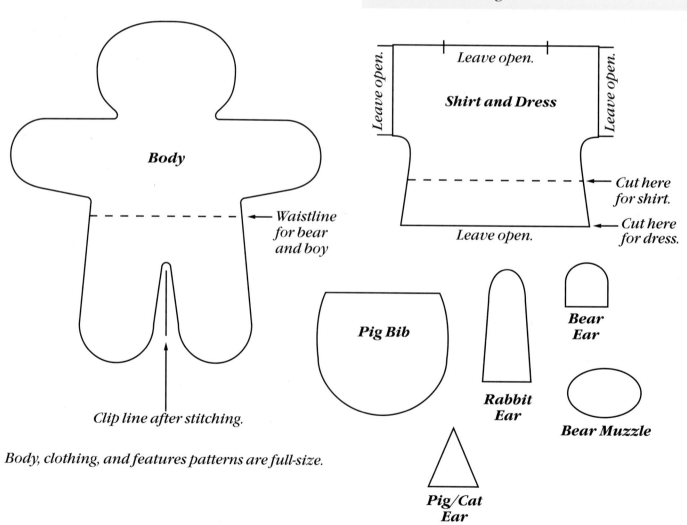

Body, clothing, and features patterns are full-size.

50

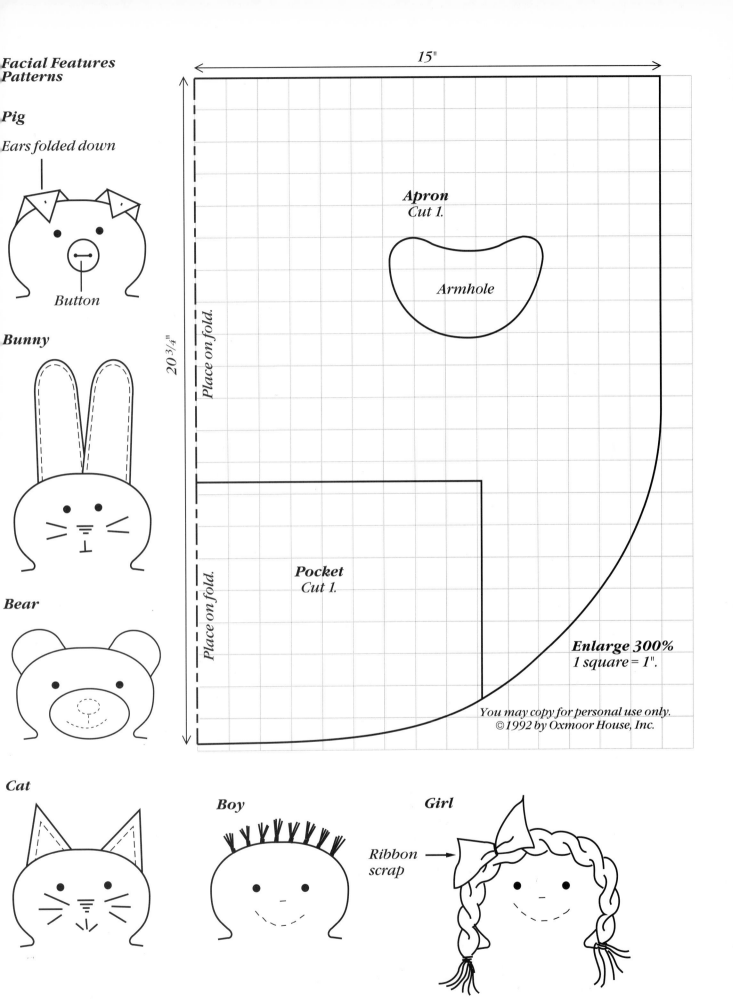

Facial Features Patterns

Pig

Ears folded down

Button

Bunny

Bear

Cat

15"

20 3/4"

Place on fold.

Place on fold.

Apron
Cut 1.

Armhole

Pocket
Cut 1.

Enlarge 300%
1 square = 1".

You may copy for personal use only.
©1992 by Oxmoor House, Inc.

Boy

Girl

Ribbon scrap →

51

Easy Doll Quilts

Doll quilts are not just for children anymore. Collecting dolls has become a passion for adults, and doll quilts are popular items at craft fairs and bazaars. These two quick quilts were made from the same pretty fabrics, using two different patterns. But, of course, you'll want lots of different colors and prints for sale at your bazaar.

Nine-Patch Doll Quilt

Finished Size: 22" square

Fabrics and Materials

Small print	¼ yard
Solid fabric	¼ yard
Large print	¼ yard
Backing	¾ yard
Batting	22½" square

9 (8") lengths of acrylic yarn

Pieces to Cut

6½" square*	5 solid
	4 small print
23½" square	1 backing
2½" x 18½" strip**	2 large print
2½" x 22½" strip**	2 large print

▶▶▶ TIME-SAVER

*You can cut these 6½" squares quickly using the rotary cutter. Referring to Rotary Cutting, page 140, cut 1 (6½" x 45"-wide) strip from solid; then cut 5 (6½") squares from the crosswise strip.

From small print, cut 1 (6½" x 45"-wide) strip; then cut 4 (6½") squares from the crosswise strip. Set aside the remainder of the strips for other projects.

**To cut border strips using the rotary cutter: From large print, cut 2 (2½" x 45"-wide) strips. From each crosswise strip, cut 1 (18½"-long) strip and 1 (22½"-long) strip.

Instructions

1. For 9-patch center, arrange and join 6½" squares to make 2 solid/small print/solid rows and 1 small print/solid/small print row. Join rows, alternating color placement to make checkerboard.

2. With right sides facing and raw edges aligned, join 2 (2½" x 18½") strips to opposite sides of quilt. Press seams toward borders. Repeat to join longer strips to remaining sides.

3. Turn under ¼" on all edges of backing and press. Place backing (right side down) on a flat surface. Center and stack batting and pieced top (right side up) on backing.

4. Fold backing to front of quilt to make a ½" self-binding. Using thread to match binding, slipstitch or machine-edgestitch binding to front of quilt, mitering corners.

5. Refer to Tying Quilts, page 148, to tie quilt with yarn bows.

BAZAAR TIP

To introduce newcomers to the fun of patchwork, sell Ready-to-Sew Doll Quilt Kits at your bazaar. Making a doll quilt on the sewing machine is an activity mothers and daughters can share. And even the very young can make a doll quilt when the pieces are sewn by hand.

Cut all of the pieces for the Nine-Patch Doll Quilt, above, and place them in a large zip-top plastic bag. Don't forget to include batting, backing, yarn, and some simple instructions for assembly.

The Pinwheel Doll Quilt that follows could also be assembled for a slightly more challenging kit. Although it will take a little longer to sew all of the triangles together, it is still a good choice for beginners.

Pinwheel Doll Quilt

Finished Size: 22" square

Fabrics and Materials

Pattern, page 152

Small print	¼ yard
Solid fabric	¼ yard
Large print	¼ yard
Backing	¾ yard
Batting	22½" square

Acrylic yarn (optional)

Pieces to Cut

Template T3*	36 solid
	36 small print
22½" square	1 backing
2½" x 18½" strip**	2 large print
2½" x 22½" strip**	2 large print

▶▶▶ TIME-SAVER

*Quick-cut these triangles without patterns, using a rotary cutter. Referring to Rotary Cutting, page140, cut 2 (3⅞" x 45"-wide) crosswise strips each of solid and small print fabrics. Cut these strips to yield 18 (3⅞") squares of each fabric.

Stack squares evenly in groups of 4 and use rotary cutter to cut stacks in half diagonally.

**Referring to rotary cutting instructions for Nine-Patch Doll Quilt, on previous page, cut border strips from large print fabric.

Instructions

1. Join long edges of 1 solid and 1 small print triangle to make a square. Repeat, joining remaining triangles to make 36 squares.

Referring to photo for placement, assemble 4 pieced squares to form pinwheel design. Make 9 pinwheel squares.

2. Join 3 pinwheel squares to make 1 row. Repeat to make 2 more rows. Join 3 rows to form 18½" square.

3. Refer to Nine-Patch Doll Quilt, Step 2, to add border strips.

4. Stack batting, top (right side up), and backing (right side down). With batting against feed dogs, join layers, leaving an opening for turning. Clip corners and turn. Slipstitch opening closed.

5. Machine-stitch in-the-ditch inside border to secure layers, or tie with yarn, as desired.

Siamese Cat Belt

Quiltmaker Betsy Freeman, of Tryon, North Carolina, was inspired by her friend, cartoonist Don Tyler, to create this friendly feline belt. When it's wrapped around a little girl's waist, the look is completed by the cat's curling black tail. The instructions given here are for a 22½-inch waist, which is just right for most five-to-seven year olds. Adding some extra fasteners would make it more adjustable. And, of course, you can make additional belts in longer lengths.

Fabrics and Materials

Patterns, page 56	
Light brown print	¼ yard
Scraps of black fabric	
Scrap of medium blue fabric	
White dressmaker's carbon	
Paper-backed fusible web	
Thread to match fabrics	
Polyester stuffing	
Fusible interfacing	
⅝" belt hook and eye fastener	

Pieces to Cut

2" x 27" strip	2 lt. brown print
2" x 6" strip	2 black
1½" x 33" strip	1 fusible interfacing

Instructions

1. Trace head pattern and cut 2 from light brown print. Cut a 2"-long horizontal slit in center of 1 head piece. Set aside.

Referring to Paper-backed Fusible Web, page 143, trace 1 face, 2 eyes, 2 pupils, and 2 ears on paper side of fusible web. Following manufacturer's instructions, fuse eyes to wrong side of blue fabric and remaining pieces to wrong side of black fabric. Cut out and remove paper backings. Use dressmaker's carbon to trace stitching lines on face for nose, mouth, and whiskers.

2. Following manufacturer's instructions, fuse pupils to center of eyes. Fuse eyes to face.

Aligning raw edges with placement line, position face on head piece without slit; fuse. Fuse ears in same manner.

3. With black thread, machine-appliqué bottom edges of ears and top edge of face. Satin-stitch along marked lines for facial features. Using blue thread and narrow zigzag, stitch around eyes. With slightly wider stitch, make a second line of stitching over the first to create appearance of eyelashes.

4. With right sides facing and raw edges aligned, stitch head front to head back, stitching completely around head. Trim corners and turn through opening in back of head. Stuff; then whipstitch slit closed.

5. With right sides facing and raw edges aligned, stitch 1 end of 1 black strip to 1 end of 1 brown strip. Repeat with remaining strips.

Center 1½" x 33" strip of interfacing on wrong side of 1 pieced strip. Following manufacturer's instructions, fuse interfacing to fabric. With right sides

facing and raw edges aligned, stitch strips together, rounding black end and leaving other end open.

Trim rounded seam. Turn and press. Turn raw edge to inside and whipstitch closed.

6. Slipstitch 3" at end of belt to back of cat's head, covering slit.

7. Referring to Diagram, tack belt hook at an angle to back of head. Measure 22½" from hook and tack eye fastener at an angle on right side of belt.

Fastener Placement

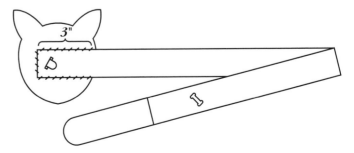

Patterns are full-size.

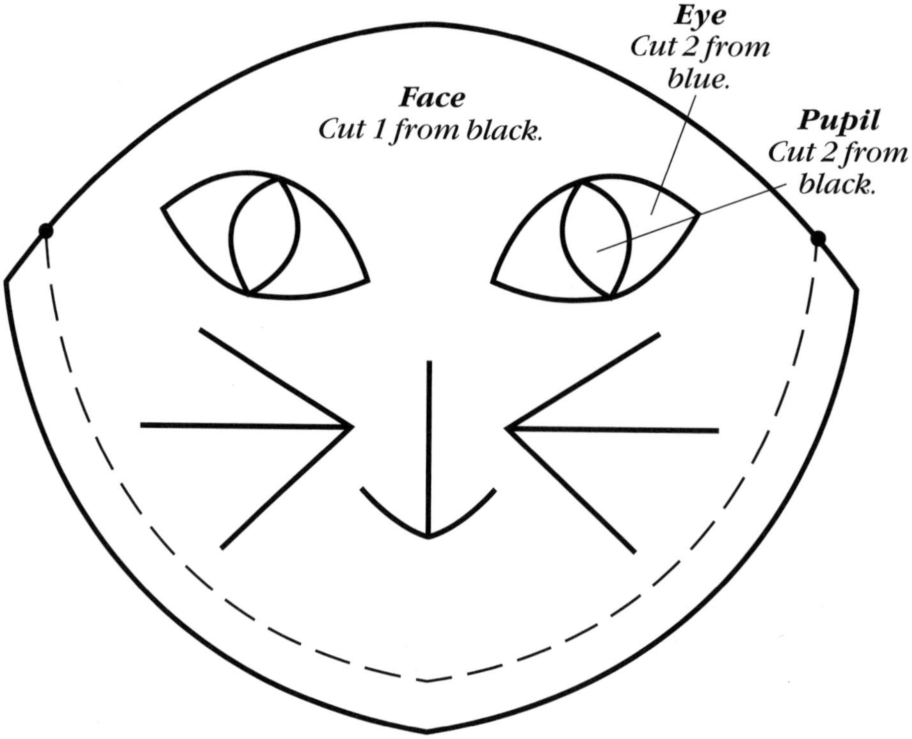

Eye
Cut 2 from blue.

Face
Cut 1 from black.

Pupil
Cut 2 from black.

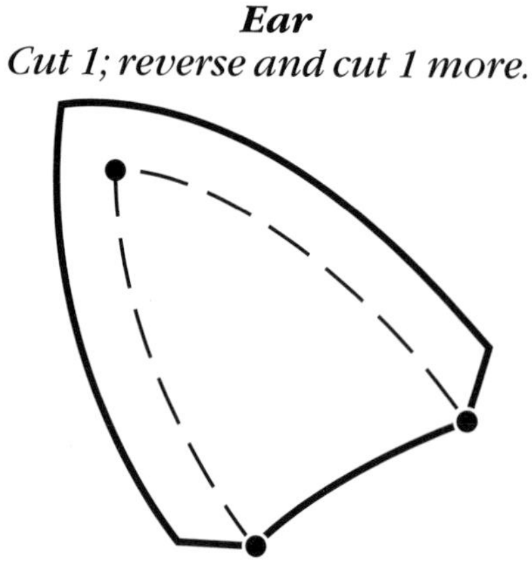

Ear
Cut 1; reverse and cut 1 more.

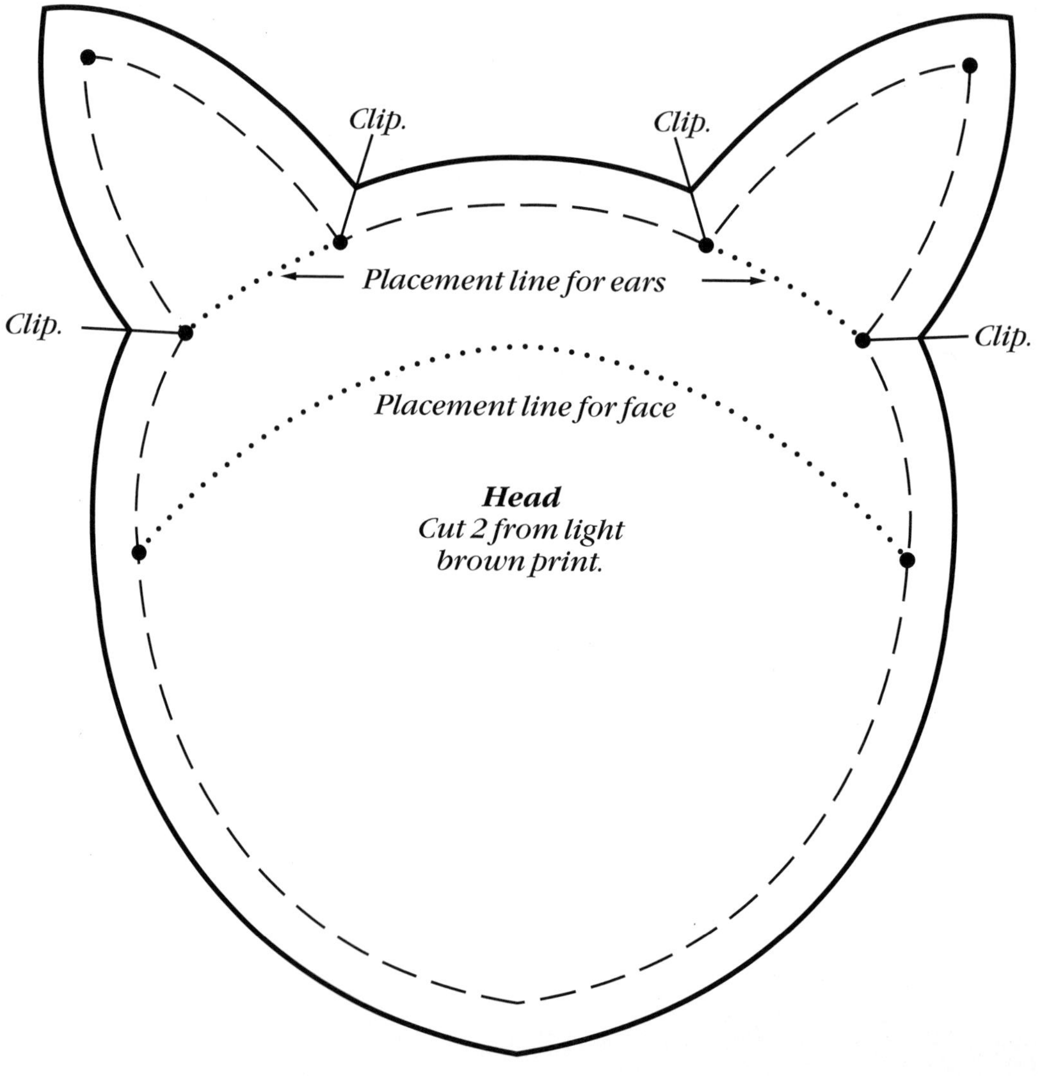

Clip.   *Clip.*

Clip. →

← — *Placement line for ears* — →

← *Clip.*

Placement line for face ·····

Head
Cut 2 from light brown print.

Wonderful Wearable Patchwork

Grandmother's Flower Garden goes modern when it's machine-appliquéd on these two bright sweatshirts. Pink hexagon flowers bloom on one, while the other will make a soccer star smile with pride. They're both so quick and easy to make that you'll want to try several color combinations.

And Priscilla Wentworth, of Searsport, Maine, has become quite well-known for her colorful, reversible patchwork caps.

Because they appeal to both boys and girls and different ages, Priscilla has provided the pattern in three sizes. Though the patchwork looks intricate, using a rotary cutter and the strip-piecing method speeds up the process.

Flower Garden Sweatshirt

Fabrics and Materials (for 1 sweatshirt)
Purchased sweatshirt
Paper-backed fusible web
Tear-away stabilizer or white paper
Scraps of pink prints, yellow prints
Blue thread

Instructions
1. Referring to Paper-backed Fusible Web, page 143, trace A 7 times and B 7 times on paper side of fusible web. Cut paper shapes apart. Following manufacturer's instructions, fuse 1 A and 1 B to wrong side of yellow print scrap. Fuse remaining shapes to wrong sides of pink print scraps. Cut out all shapes and remove paper backings.
2. Referring to photo for placement, position As for large flower. Fuse in place. Position Bs for small flower and fuse.
3. Place a piece of tear-away stabilizer or paper behind appliqué. Referring to Machine Appliqué, page 143, and using blue thread, start stitching at 1 corner of center hexagon. Stop at next corner, with needle down. Raise presser foot, turn sweatshirt, lower presser foot, and stitch away from center between 2 pink print hexagons, ending stitching at outside edge. Clip threads. Start stitching again at center hexagon where direction of stitching changed, and proceed in same manner until all sides of center hexagon and all adjacent edges of pink print hexagons have been stitched.

With machine needle down and pivoting at each corner, complete stitching around outside edge.

Repeat to machine-appliqué second flower.
4. Remove paper or stabilizer.

Soccer Star Sweatshirt

Fabrics and Materials (for 1 sweatshirt)
Purchased sweatshirt
Paper-backed fusible web
Tear-away stabilizer or white paper
Scraps of cream print, black print,
    red print, gold print
Red thread

Instructions
1. Referring to Paper-backed Fusible Web, page 143, trace A 7 times on paper side of fusible web. Cut paper shapes apart. Fuse 6 As to wrong side of cream print and 1 A to wrong side of black print. Trace C 6 times on paper side of fusible web and fuse to wrong side of black print. Using pattern for Star # 2, page 156, trace star 2 times on paper side of fusible web and fuse to wrong side of 1 red print and 1 gold print.

Cut out all shapes and remove paper backings.
2. Referring to photo for placement, position black print center hexagon of soccer ball. (Complete ball will be 7½" in diameter.) Following manufacturer's instructions, fuse center hexagon. Aligning 1 raw edge of black hexagon with 1 edge of each cream print hexagon, position cream print hexagons and fuse in place. Aligning raw edges, position Cs around edge of ball and fuse.

Referring to photo for placement, position red print and gold print stars and fuse in place.
3. Referring to Flower Garden Sweatshirt, Step 3, and using red thread, appliqué hexagons of soccer ball in same manner. Machine-appliqué inside edges of all Cs. Complete appliqué around outside of soccer ball.

Machine-appliqué stars.
4. Remove paper or stabilizer.

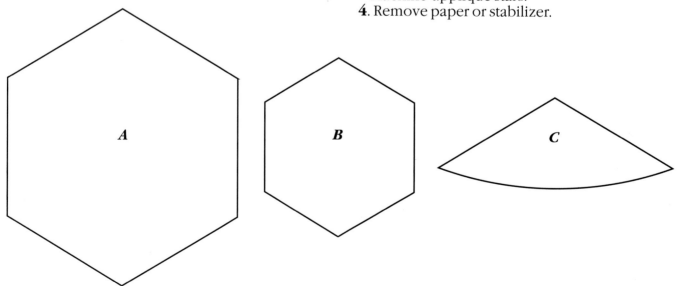

Patchwork Cap

Fabrics and Materials

Patterns, page 61-63
Tracing paper
Royal blue   ¼ yard
Aqua   ¼ yard
Med. blue   ¼ yard
Red   ⅛ yard
Lavender   ⅛ yard
Quilter's ruler
Rotary cutter and mat
Fusible interfacing
4" (⅜"-wide) elastic
1 package of 1"-wide aqua double-fold bias tape

▶▶▶ TIME-SAVER

Instead of piecing the patchwork for these caps, you can save time by using ½ yard of a pre-printed patchwork fabric. Since the caps are reversible, choose bright coordinating scraps for the lining pieces. Use the same patterns and instructions, omitting the steps for assembling the patchwork.

Pieces to Cut

2¾" x 24¾"	1 royal
	1 aqua
2½" x 37½"	1 royal
	1 med. blue
2½" x 25"	1 red
	1 lavender
1¼" x 7½" strip	2 lavender
	1 red
	2 med. blue
	1 royal
1¼" x 3¾" strip	2 red
	2 aqua
	2 royal
Template A (lining crown)	2 royal (lining)
Template B (sides)	2 patchwork
	2 aqua (lining)
Template C (visor)	1 patchwork
	1 med. blue (lining)
	2 fusible interfacing
Template D (center crown)	2 patchwork
Template E (crown end)	4 patchwork

Instructions

1. Select cap size and make templates of all pattern pieces. Cut out templates and set aside.
2. To assemble patchwork: Referring to Diagram A, Figure 1 for colors and dimensions, join sets of strips lengthwise as shown. Press all seams open. Cut across pieced bands at 2½" intervals as shown to form pieced units. Assemble pieced units into rows. Make 3 of Row A; make 2 of Row B.

Diagram A: Patchwork Assembly
Figure 1

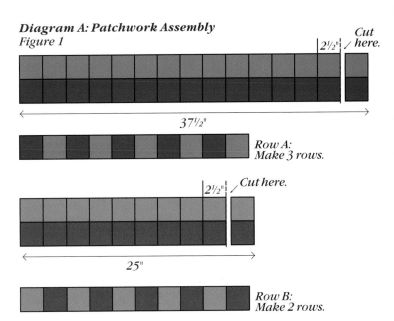

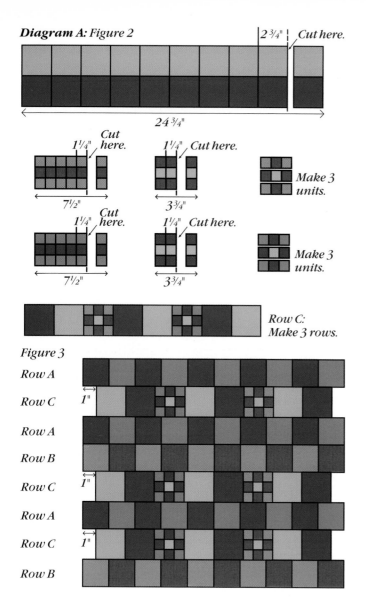

Diagram A: Figure 2

2 ¾" | Cut here.

24 ¾"

Cut here. 1¼"

Cut here. 1¼"

7½" 3¾"

Make 3 units.

Cut here. 1¼"

Cut here. 1¼"

7½" 3¾"

Make 3 units.

Row C: Make 3 rows.

Figure 3

Row A

Row C   1"

Row A

Row B

Row C   1"

Row A

Row C   1"

Row B

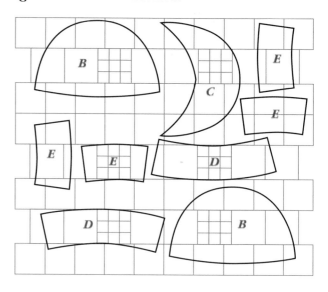

Diagram B: Pattern Placement

B

C

E

E

E

E

D

D

B

For Row C, referring to Figure 2, join aqua/royal strip lengthwise as shown. Cut across pieced band at 2¾" intervals. Set aside.

Join 1¼" strips as shown. Cut across pieced bands at 1¼" intervals to make pieced units. Make 3 lavender/red/aqua 9-patch blocks, and 3 blue/royal/aqua 9-patch blocks, as shown in Figure 2. Assemble 9-patch blocks and aqua/royal units in a row as shown. Repeat to make 2 more Row Cs.

Referring to Figure 3 for placement, assemble patchwork rows, offsetting Row Cs as shown.

3. Arrange templates on patchwork as shown in Diagram B. Trace and cut out all pieces.

4. With right sides facing and raw edges aligned, join 1 E to each end of 1 D. Referring to Diagram C, Figure 1, compare length of patchwork crown unit with lining piece A. Trim patchwork to match, if necessary. Repeat.

With right sides facing and raw edges aligned, pin 1 patchwork crown unit to 1 patchwork piece B and stitch. Repeat. Join these units together along curved center seam. (See Figure 2.) Assemble lining units A and B in same manner.

5. Following manufacturer's instructions, fuse 1 interfacing to wrong side of patchwork piece C and 1 interfacing to wrong side of lining piece C.

With wrong sides facing, and raw edges aligned, baste Cs together to form visor. Use bias tape to bind outer edge of visor. Mark center of inner curve of visor.

6. With right sides facing, match center of visor with center seam of patchwork crown and pin. Join visor to crown, using a scant ¼" seam. Remove pins and basting.

With right sides facing, match center of visor lining with center of cap lining and pin. With right sides facing and referring to Figure 3, pin lining to patchwork cap, matching side and crown seams. Beginning at 1 side back seam and using ¼" seam, stitch around cap, catching visor in seam. Continue stitching to other side back seam, leaving space between back side seams open. Turn through opening. Turn under raw edges ¼" and press.

7. To insert elastic at back of cap: Referring to Diagram D, Figure 1, measure ¾" up from bottom edge of cap at both side back seams and mark. Topstitch a horizontal line between marks. Insert elastic between patchwork and lining, extending right end of elastic ½" beyond side back seam. Pin elastic in place through patchwork. Stitch from end of topstitching line along seam line to raw edge of cap, catching end of elastic in seam.

Referring to Figure 2, position other end of elastic, pin, and stitch in same manner. Turn under raw edges and slipstitch bottom edges closed.

On right side of cap, starting at 1 side back seam, edgestitch through all layers along cap edge, continuing around cap to other side back seam.

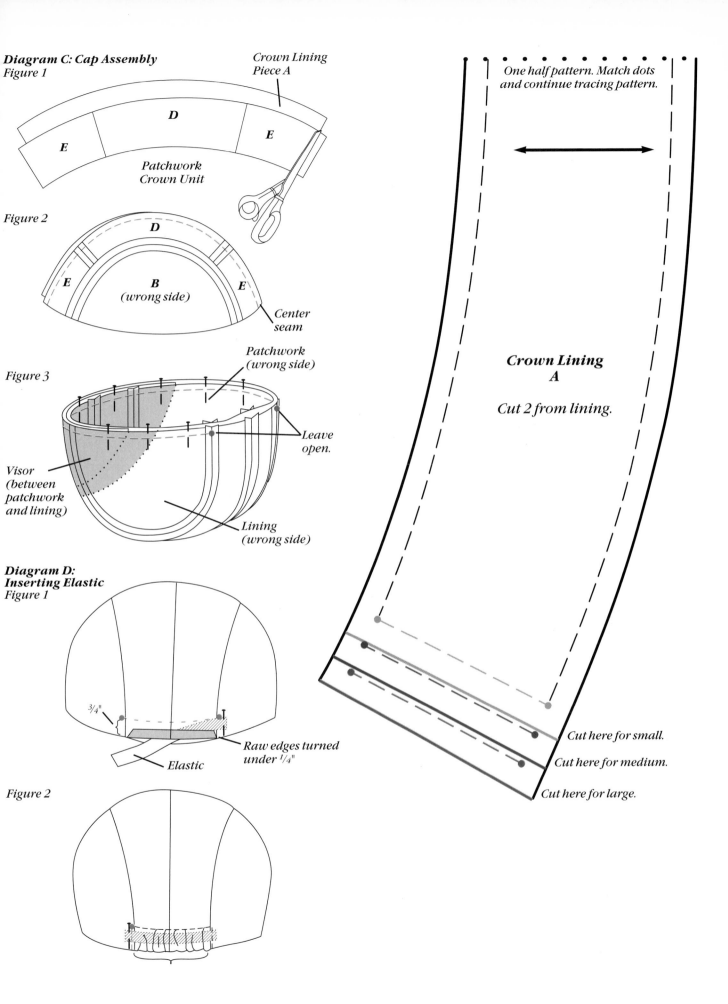

Diagram C: Cap Assembly
Figure 1

Crown Lining
Piece A

D

E

E

Patchwork
Crown Unit

Figure 2

D

E

B
(wrong side)

E

Center
seam

Figure 3

Patchwork
(wrong side)

Leave
open.

Visor
(between
patchwork
and lining)

Lining
(wrong side)

**Diagram D:
Inserting Elastic**
Figure 1

3/4"

Raw edges turned
under 1/4"

Elastic

Figure 2

One half pattern. Match dots
and continue tracing pattern.

*Crown Lining
A*

Cut 2 from lining.

Cut here for small.

Cut here for medium.

Cut here for large.

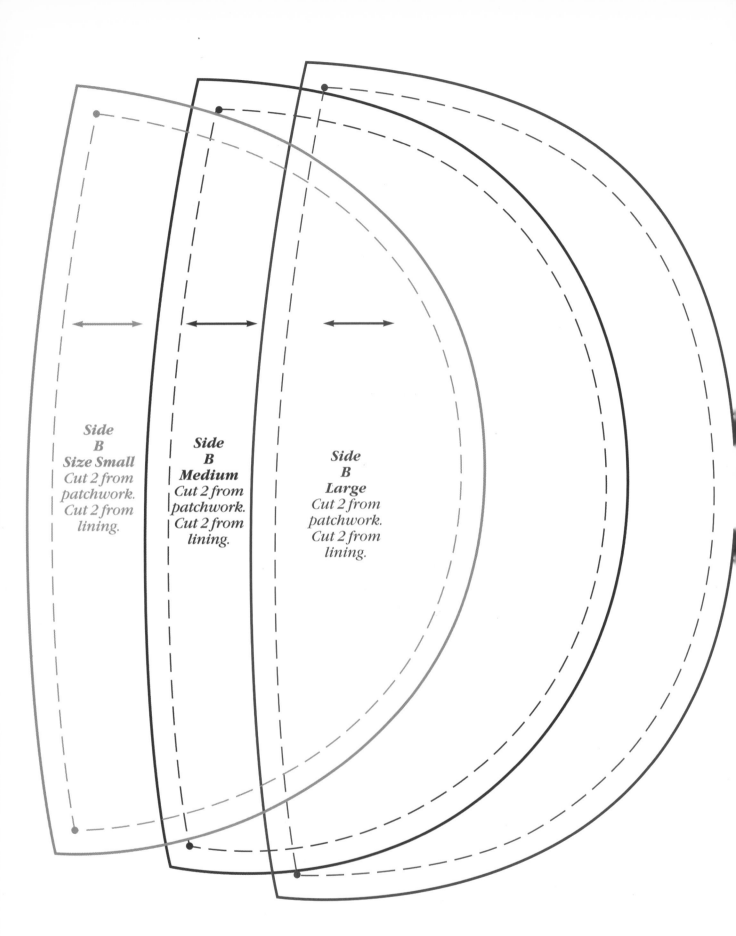

Side
B
Size Small
Cut 2 from patchwork.
Cut 2 from lining.

Side
B
Medium
Cut 2 from patchwork.
Cut 2 from lining.

Side
B
Large
Cut 2 from patchwork.
Cut 2 from lining.

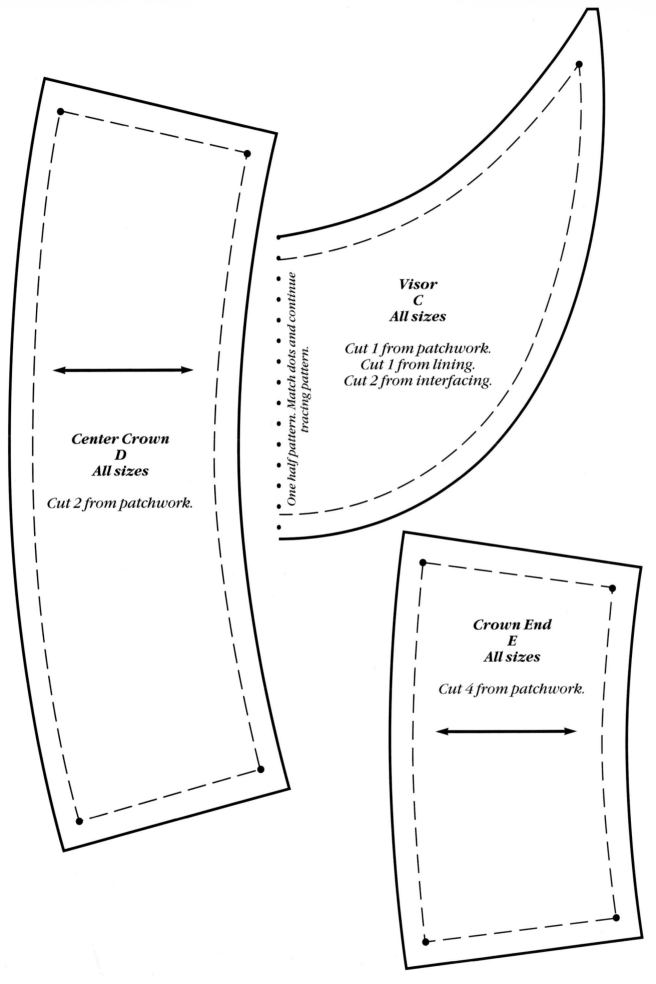

Center Crown
D
All sizes

Cut 2 from patchwork.

Visor
C
All sizes

Cut 1 from patchwork.
Cut 1 from lining.
Cut 2 from interfacing.

One half pattern. Match dots and continue tracing pattern.

Crown End
E
All sizes

Cut 4 from patchwork.

Sunbonnet Sam Set

This *Sunbonnet Sam* set was designed just for little boys by Ginger Kean Berk, of Ambler, Pennsylvania. For the quilt, she chose country combinations of soft denim and folksy gingham and put them on a crisp white background that makes the colors shine. Sam's accessories include a large laundry bag that will be right at home in a little boy's room or that can go along for a few days' visit to Grandma's house. And there's a cute pajama bag that can double as a pillow.

Some projects, like this quilt, can be sold as "special orders," which means that your bazaar can continue to raise money after the event is over. Any item that takes too much time to be made in multiples can be ordered for delivery at a later time.

Materials for All Pieces
Paper-backed fusible web
Tear-away stabilizer or white paper

Quilt

Finished Size
Quilt: 55" x 76"
Blocks: 12 (10" x 12")

Fabrics and Materials
Pattern, page 66	
White fabric	4½ yards
Lt. blue denim	2¼ yards
12 assorted denim solids	8" x 11" scrap each
6 assorted ginghams	¼ yard each
White piping	7½ yards
Threads to match denim solids	
8 assorted colors of yarn	1½ yards each
2½" square of cardboard	
Thick batting	1 twin size

Pieces to Cut
10½" x 12½" rectangle	12 white

Note: Cut rectangles lengthwise end to end along 1 selvage edge of fabric. Remainder of white will be pieced for backing.

3½" x 10½" strip	9 lt. blue denim
3½" x 57½" strip	4 lt. blue denim
3½" x 42½" strip	2 lt. blue denim
5" x 65½" strip	2 lt. blue denim
5" x 53½" strip	2 lt. blue denim
1½" x 3½" strips	27 each of 6 ginghams

Instructions
Hint: Ginger suggests that you spray-starch and press your fabrics after washing them. It makes fabric easier to cut and sew accurately. As the quilt is handled during construction, the stiffness of starching disappears.

1. Referring to Paper-backed Fusible Web, page 143, use patterns on page 66 to trace each piece (hat/overalls, shirt, hatband, and pocket) 12 times on paper side of fusible web. Cut web pieces apart.

Fuse pieces to wrong sides of fabric—hat/overalls to solids, and shirt, hatband, and pocket to gingham. Cut out pieces.

2. Select pieces for 1 Sam and remove paper backings. Center 1 hat/overalls on 1 white rectangle, positioning shirt beneath overalls. Following manufacturer's instructions, fuse in place. Referring to pattern for placement, fuse hatband and pocket in place. Repeat for remaining blocks.

3. Referring to Machine Appliqué, page 143, place stabilizer behind block. Using thread to match color of hat/overalls, machine-appliqué around each piece. Remove stabilizer. Repeat for remaining blocks.

4. Referring to Diagram on page 66, join 4 blocks with 3 (3½" x 10½") sashing strips to make 1 vertical row. Repeat to make 2 more rows.

Join rows with 4 (3½" x 57½") sashing strips as shown in diagram. Join 3½" x 42½" strips to top and bottom of quilt.

5. To make multi-colored borders: Using random color placement, join 21 (1½" x 3½") gingham strips end to end to make 1 (63"-long) side border. Repeat. Join pieced borders to sides of quilt, trimming to fit if necessary.

Join 15 strips in same manner to make 1 (45"-long) top border. Repeat for bottom border. Join to quilt.

6. Join 5" x 65½" denim strips to sides of quilt. Join 5" x 53½" strips to top and bottom of quilt.

7. Referring to Step 5, piece 2 (76"-long) side borders with 26 gingham strips each. Join to sides of quilt, trimming ends if necessary. Piece 2 (57"-long) borders with 19 pieces each and join to top and bottom of quilt.

8. With right sides facing, raw edges aligned, and piping facing center of quilt, join piping to quilt top, rounding corners slightly.

9. To make backing: Piece lengths of remaining white fabric together and press seam to 1 side. Trim backing and batting to match quilt top.

10. Layer batting, backing (right side up), and top (right side down). With batting against feed dogs, join layers along all sides, sewing on stitching line of piping and leaving about 12" open for turning. Turn quilt. Slipstitch opening closed.

11. Referring to Machine Quilting, page 150, machine-quilt in-the-ditch around all blocks and sashing.

12. Make 20 yarn bows as follows: Wind yarn around cardboard 8 times. Remove from cardboard. Tie yarn in center. Referring to photo for placement and using matching thread, tack bows between blocks.

Quilt Top Assembly

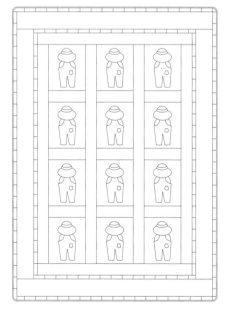

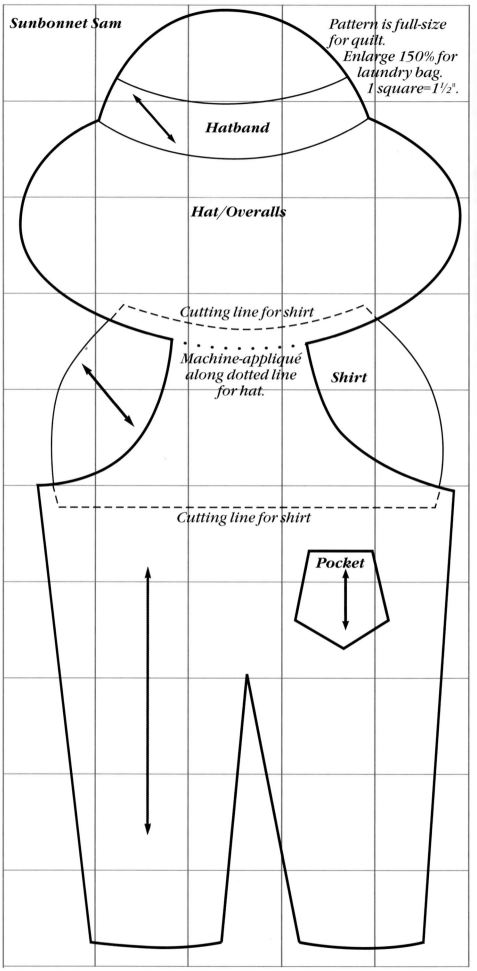

Sunbonnet Sam

Pattern is full-size for quilt.
Enlarge 150% for laundry bag.
1 square=1½".

Hatband

Hat/Overalls

Cutting line for shirt

Machine-appliqué along dotted line for hat.

Shirt

Cutting line for shirt

Pocket

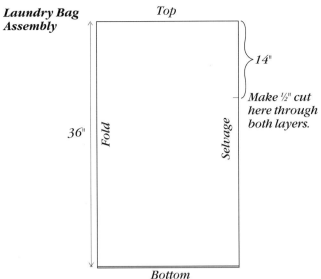

Laundry Bag Assembly

Top

14"

36" Fold Selvage

Make ½" cut here through both layers.

Bottom

down to horizontal cut and press. Topstitch hem. Repeat on other side.

2. On top edge of fabric, turn under ½" and then 3" and press. Using red thread, stitch across fabric close to first folded edge. To make casing, stitch again 1¼" above first stitching.

3. Enlarge Sunbonnet Sam pattern.

4. Trace hat/overalls, shirt, pocket, and hatband on paper side of fusible web. Cut apart. Following manufacturer's instructions, fuse pieces to wrong side of fabrics—hat/overalls to red denim, and shirt, pocket, and hatband to blue gingham. Cut out pieces and remove paper backings.

On paper side of remaining fusible web, draw 2 (6") squares. Cut each square in half diagonally, making 4 paper triangles. Fuse 1 triangle each to red denim, blue gingham, red gingham, and dark blue solid. Cut out all triangles and remove paper backings.

5. With wrong sides facing, re-fold bag in half widthwise. Center hat/overalls on bag, with bottom of overalls approximately 7½" from bottom raw edge. Position shirt under overalls, and hatband and pocket in place. Fuse to bag.

Referring to photo, arrange triangles below Sam, with long edges of triangles 2½" from bottom of bag and overlapping each triangle 5" at sides. Fuse triangles in place. Unfold bag.

6. Referring to Machine Appliqué, page 143, place stabilizer behind Sam and triangles. Using red thread, machine-appliqué around each piece. Remove stabilizer.

7. With right sides facing and raw edges aligned, re-fold bag in half widthwise. Using a ½" seam, stitch across bottom and up side to bottom of finished opening. Zigzag raw edges of seam allowance together. Press seams to 1 side.

Turn bag right side out. Satin-stitch across bottom edge of side opening to reinforce.

8. Thread cord through casing. Knot ends together.

Laundry Bag

Fabrics and Materials

Pattern, page 66

Lt. blue denim	1 yard
Red denim	¼ yard
Blue gingham	¼ yard

Scraps of red gingham, dk. blue fabrics
Red, blue thread
2 yards of ⅝"-diameter red cord

Instructions

1. With wrong sides facing, fold light blue denim in half widthwise, selvage to selvage. To hem opening on top right side of laundry bag, measure 14" down from top edge and make ½" horizontal cut through both selvage edges (see Diagram). Unfold fabric. On 1 side, turn 14" segment under ¼" twice

Pajama Bag

Fabrics and Materials

Tracing paper
Red denim ⅔ yard
Blue gingham ¼ yard
Red thread
Muslin ⅓ yard
Thin batting
Scrap of fusible interfacing
9" red zipper
6" (¼"-wide) red grosgrain ribbon

Pieces to Cut

10" x 18" rectangle — 1 denim (hat/overalls)
12" x 20" rectangle — 2 denim (front and back)
2 muslin (lining)
2 batting
2" x 10" strip — 1 denim (zipper placket)

Instructions

1. Using tracing paper and matching dots, trace complete pajama bag pattern. (See page 69.)
2. Trace hat/overalls, shirt, and hatband onto paper side of fusible web. Cut apart. Following manufacturer's instructions, fuse to wrong side of fabrics—hat/overalls to 10" x 18" denim rectangle, and shirt and hatband to blue gingham. Cut out. Remove paper backings.
3. Center hat/overalls on right side of 1 denim rectangle. Referring to pattern for placement, position shirt underneath overalls and hatband on hat. Fuse in place.

Trace pocket pattern on right side of blue gingham. Following manufacturer's instructions, fuse wrong side of gingham to fusible interfacing. Cut out on marked line. Satin-stitch top edge of pocket. Referring to pattern for position, pin pocket to overalls.

Referring to Machine Appliqué, page 143, place stabilizer on wrong side of denim behind appliqués. Machine-appliqué around each piece, leaving top edge of pocket open and continuing line of stitching around hat brim. Remove stabilizer.
4. Stack 1 muslin lining, batting, and appliquéd denim rectangle (right side up) and pin. Referring to Diagram A, topstitch along outside edges of machine-appliqué stitching and from center bottom of leg straight up for 4" as shown. Set aside.
5. To insert zipper in bag back: Zigzag edges of 2" x 10" zipper placket. On wrong side of strip, draw a line lengthwise down center. Using this line to center, draw a ½" x 8¾" rectangle. (See Diagram B, Figure 1.)

Stack remaining muslin lining, batting, and denim rectangle (right side up) and pin. With right sides facing, center placket on denim rectangle. Pin strip to rectangle. Referring to Figure 2, topstitch

Diagram A:
Bag Front Assembly

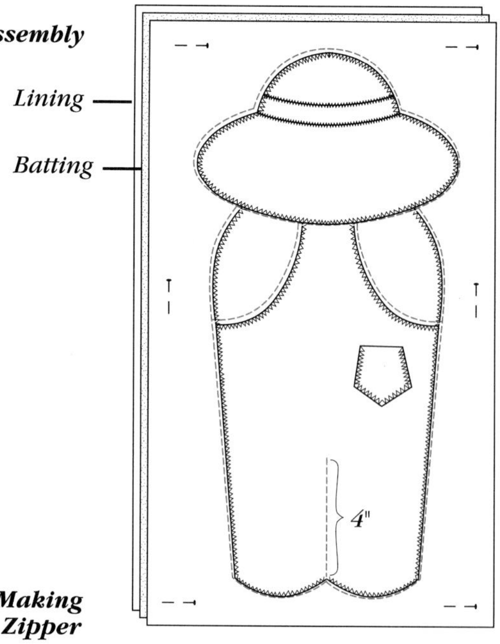

Lining

Batting

4"

Diagram B: Making
Opening for Zipper
Figure 1

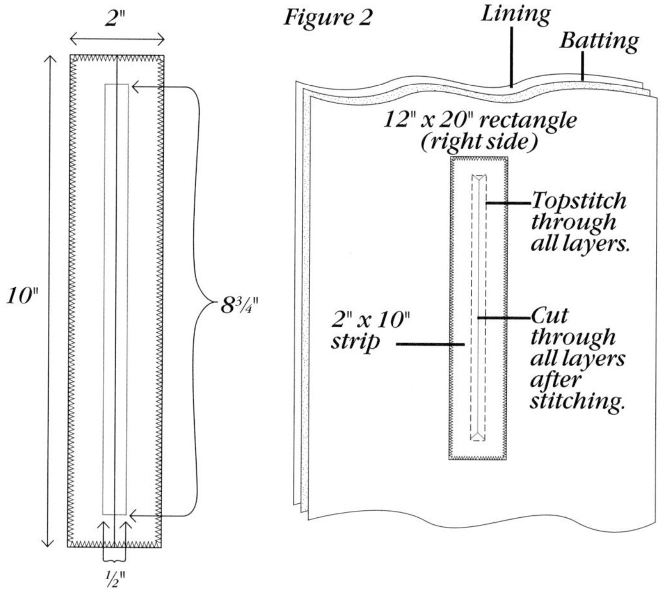

2"

10"

8¾"

½"

Figure 2 — Lining

Batting

12" x 20" rectangle
(right side)

Topstitch through all layers.

2" x 10" strip

Cut through all layers after stitching.

along marked rectangle lines on placket. Cutting through all layers, cut along center line and from center line to each corner as shown. Turn placket to lining side through cut opening. Press.

With right side of zipper facing lining, center zipper behind placket and opening. Topstitch in place close to folded edge of opening. Then topstitch completely around zipper ½" from previous zipper stitching. Open zipper.
6. With right sides facing, center appliquéd front rectangle on back rectangle. Pin. Using topstitching outline on appliquéd front as a guide, stitch all the way around outline.
7. Trim seam allowance to ½". Trim batting close to seam. Clip ¼" into corners and curves. Zigzag raw edges of seam allowances together. Turn bag through zipper opening.
8. Tie ribbon to zipper pull.

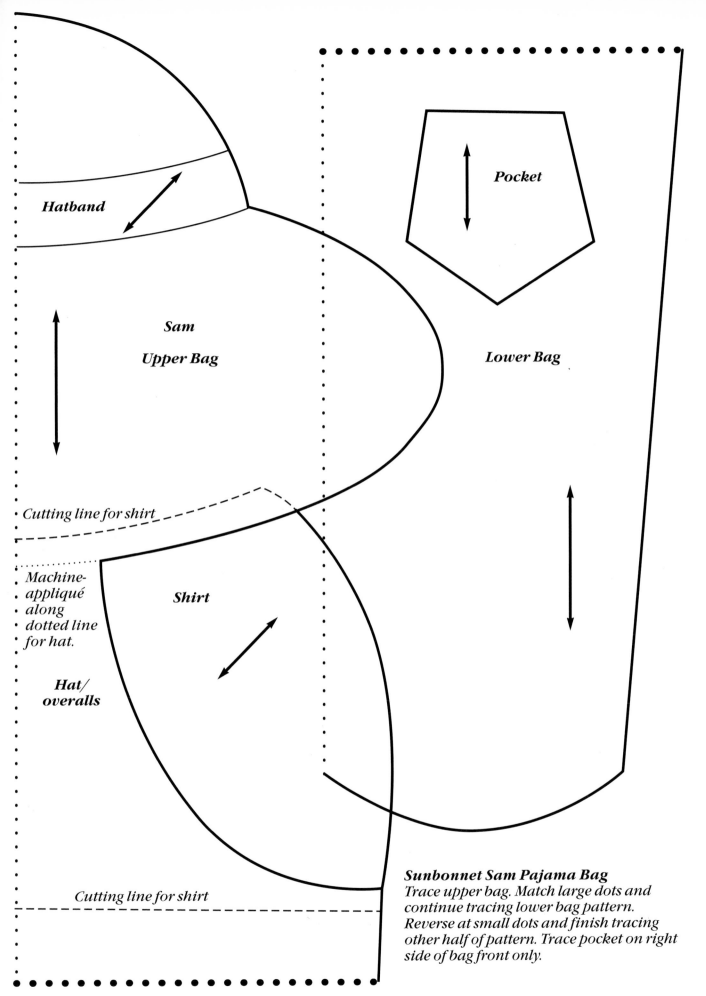

Hatband

Sam

Upper Bag

Pocket

Lower Bag

Cutting line for shirt

Machine-appliqué along dotted line for hat.

Hat/ overalls

Shirt

Cutting line for shirt

Sunbonnet Sam Pajama Bag
Trace upper bag. Match large dots and continue tracing lower bag pattern. Reverse at small dots and finish tracing other half of pattern. Trace pocket on right side of bag front only.

Fabrics and Materials
3" x 34" strip of fabric
8 (10-mm or larger) wooden or pony beads
7 marbles

Instructions
1. With right sides facing and raw edges aligned, fold fabric in half lengthwise. Referring to Diagram, stitch, leaving an opening for turning. Trim end triangles, leaving ¼" seam allowances, and turn. Press.

Diagram: Stitching Fabric Strip

Fold

Stitching line | *Leave open.*

2" | 1½" 2"

Hint: Start turning by tucking in point farthest from opening. Insert a chopstick or knitting needle into tucked part and use it to turn strip through opening.

2. Thread 1 bead on strip and then slip a marble inside fabric through opening. Continue alternating beads and marbles, ending with bead, to fill center of strip. Leave ends of strip even for ties. Slipstitch opening closed.

BAZAAR TIP
Young bazaargoers really enjoy getting involved with hands-on activities. A table for making these necklaces can be one of the most popular places at your bazaar.

Have a selection of beads, marbles, and prepared fabric strips so that young customers can assemble their own necklaces. Be sure to include some strips made from bright neon fabrics!

Prices for the finished necklaces could be based on how many beads and marbles are used. You should have a volunteer or two ready to sew up the opening on the finished necklaces, but your customers may find that it's more fun to do their own sewing.

Fabric Necklaces

According to Arleen Boyd of Rochester, New York, these colorful, easy necklaces first became popular among the members of quilt guilds in that area. The quilters wore them to meetings and quilt shows, but their young daughters really had fun with them. Nothing could be easier than alternating beads and marbles on a strip of fabric (and what a great use for those long strips left over from rotary cutting).

Party Bibs for Boys and Girls

Parents and grandparents will love these dress-up bibs with their cummerbunds and festive details, made by Judy Biber of Charlotte, North Carolina. Judy discovered that the polyester satins and other fabrics that she used for sewing prom dresses wash well and make stunning decorative accents. She cautions, however, that you should always wash and dry these fabrics to check for shrinkage or fading before using them for bibs.

Boy's Party Bib

Fabrics and Materials
Patterns, pages 72 and 73
White terry cloth ⅓ yard
7" x 8" scrap of white cotton piqué
7" x 9" scrap of red polyester satin
Black, red thread
⅜"-wide black grosgrain ribbon ½ yard
⅝"-wide lace with black edging ½ yard
1 package of ¼"-wide black double-fold bias tape

Instructions
1. On wrong side of terry cloth, trace complete bib base pattern and cut 2. On wrong side of cotton piqué, trace complete shirt front pattern and cut 1.
2. Position shirt front (right side up) on 1 bib base, aligning raw edges at neck, and pin. Pin lace along raw edges of shirt front, making a small pleat at bottom center point. Machine-baste. Trim excess lace.

Referring to photo and shirt front pattern for placement and using black thread, machine-satin-stitch 2 circles for buttons and topstitch lines to simulate tucks. If you prefer to use hand embroidery, refer to Embroidery Stitches, page 145, for satin stitch and backstitch. (Use 3 strands of black embroidery floss.)

Fold grosgrain ribbon in half to form a V. Lay ribbon over raw edges of lace and shirt front and pin. Using matching thread, edgestitch ribbon in place along both long edges. Trim excess ribbon.

3. From red satin, cut 1 (4¾" x 8¼") rectangle. With wrong sides facing, fold in half lengthwise. Aligning raw edges at bottom, pin folded satin to bib front.

4. With wrong sides facing and raw edges aligned, pin bib front to back. Edgestitch around entire bib.

5. Cut 30" of double-fold bias tape. Starting at corner of neck opening, bind outside edges of bib.

Cut 34" of bias tape and center tape on neckline. To make ties and bind neckline: Begin at 1 end of bias tape and stitch long edges together; bind raw edge of neckline in stitching and continue stitching to end of tie. Knot each end of tie.

6. To make bow tie: From red satin, cut 1 (1½" x 7") strip. With wrong sides facing, fold in half widthwise. Stitch 2 sides, leaving 1 end open for turning. Turn. Slipstitch opening closed. With red thread, gather center to form bow. Cut a 1¼" square of satin, fold under in ¼" on 2 sides and wrap around center of bow. Tack raw ends to back of bow. Tack bow to neck at center of bib.

Girl's Party Bib

Fabrics and Materials

White terry cloth	⅓ yard
4" x 8" scrap of white cotton piqué	
5" x 9" scrap of plaid polyester satin	
Red thread	
⅜"-wide red grosgrain ribbon	½ yard
⅝"-wide lace with red edging	½ yard
1 package of ¼"-wide red double-fold bias tape	
6" scrap of 1½"-wide ribbon-tiered lace	
13" scrap of ¼"-wide red satin ribbon	
1 large red satin rosette with leaves	

Instructions

1. Referring to Boy's Party Bib, Step 1, cut out 2 terry cloth bib bases. Trace collar pattern on white cotton piqué and cut 1.

2. Position collar (right side up) on 1 bib base, aligning raw edges at neck, and pin. Pin ⅝"-wide lace along raw edge of collar. Machine-baste. Trim excess lace.

Lay grosgrain ribbon along edge of collar, overlapping raw edges of collar and lace. Using

matching thread, edgestitch ribbon at top and bottom edges.

3. Referring to Boy's Party Bib, Steps 3–5, assemble bib.

4. To make corsage: Run a gathering thread along 1 long edge of 6" scrap of ribbon-tiered lace. Pull to gather in circle. Tie ¼" red satin ribbon in a bow and tack to circle. Tack large satin rosette in center of bow. Tack corsage to bib.

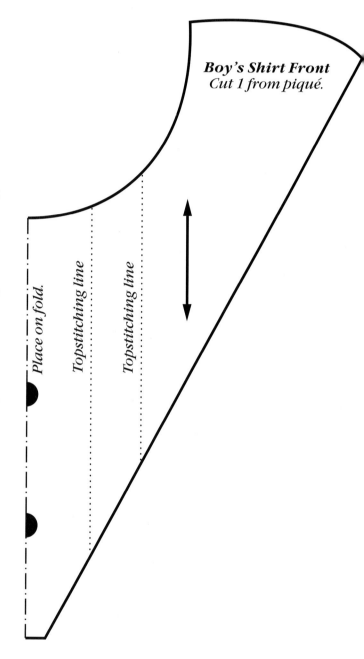

Boy's Shirt Front
Cut 1 from piqué.

Place on fold.

Topstitching line

Topstitching line

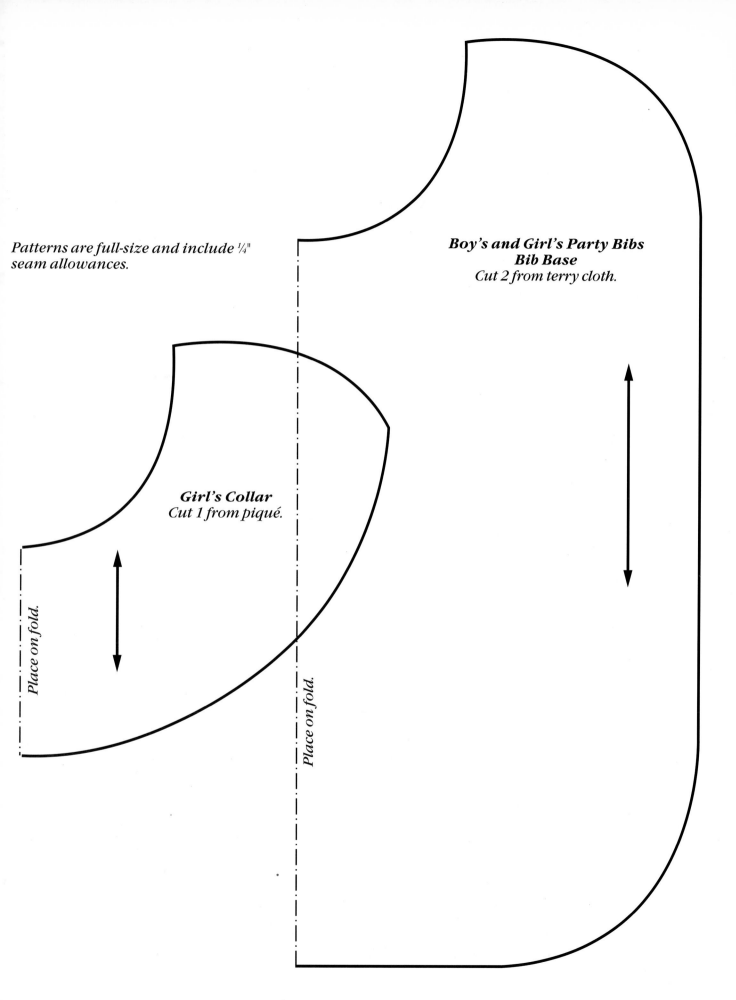

*Patterns are full-size and include ¼"
seam allowances.*

**Boy's and Girl's Party Bibs
Bib Base**
Cut 2 from terry cloth.

Girl's Collar
Cut 1 from piqué.

Place on fold.

Place on fold.

Stenciled Crib Quilt

Stencils cut from freezer paper help streamline the stenciling of this crib quilt. Since a freezer paper stencil is adhered to each block, no repositioning is required. Get some freezer paper at your grocery store and try it, experimenting with different fabric prints for the background.

Finished size
Quilt: 42" x 52"
Blocks: 20 (8") blocks

Fabrics and Materials
Pattern, page 156
White print	1 yard
Lt. blue print	⅔ yard
Lt. green print	¼ yard
Print for backing	1½ yards
Batting	1 crib-size sheet
2"-wide double-tiered ruffled lace	5¾ yards
⅜"-wide satin ribbon:	1¾ yards each
blue, pink, green, lavender	
Threads to match fabrics	

Materials for stenciling
Freezer paper
Stapler
Craft knife
Scissors
Fabric paints: blue, pink, green, lavender
A shallow dish
Stencil brushes or sponges
A smooth, flat surface for stenciling

▶▶▶ **TIME-SAVER**
You can speed through cutting the pieces for the quilt by using the rotary cutter. From white print, cut 4 (8½" x 45") crosswise strips. Cut each of these strips to yield 5 (8½" squares).

From light blue print, cut 10 (2½" x 45") crosswise strips. From 9 of these strips, cut 5 (2½" x 8½") strips. From remaining strip, cut 4 (2½" x 8½") strips.

From light green print, cut 2 (2½" x 45") crosswise strips. From each strip, cut 15 (2½" squares).

Pieces to Cut
8½" square	20 white print
8" square	20 freezer paper
2½" x 8½" strip	49 lt. blue print
2½" square	30 lt. green print
12" lengths	5 blue ribbon
	5 pink ribbon
	5 green ribbon
	5 lavender ribbon

Instructions
1. On dull side of 5 (8") squares of freezer paper, trace Heart #3. With shiny sides down and with marked square on top, make 5 stacks each of 4 freezer paper squares. Staple squares together at corners and in center of each edge.

To cut out stencils: Using a craft knife, cut out heart, cutting through all layers. Discard hearts. Using scissors, trim off edges of freezer paper squares to remove staples.

With shiny side down, center heart stencil on 8½" white print square. Press stencil onto fabric with hot, dry iron, making sure that edges around cutout heart adhere to fabric. Repeat to prepare all squares.

2. Pour small amount of fabric paint in a shallow dish.
Note: After dipping brush in paint, be sure to dab it on paper towels to remove excess paint. The brush should be almost dry.

Working with 1 color at a time as described in Stenciling, page 143, stencil blocks as follows: 5 blue, 5 pink, 5 lavender, and 5 green.

3. When all stenciling is complete and paint is dry, peel away freezer paper. To heat-set paint, press block on wrong side, using a hot, dry iron and a press cloth.

4. Referring to photo, join 5 (2½") squares and 4 (2½" x 8½") strips to make 1 row of sashing. Repeat to make 6 horizontal rows.

Join 5 (2½" x 8½") strips to sides of 4 blocks, alternating colors of hearts as desired, to make 5 (4-block) horizontal rows.

Assemble quilt top as shown in photo.

5. Measure top and cut backing to match.

6. With right sides facing and raw edges aligned, pin lace to quilt top, allowing extra fullness at corners. Using a scant ¼" seam, stitch completely around edge.

7. Layer batting, top (right side up), and backing (right side down). With batting against feed dogs, stitch layers on all sides, leaving 12" open for turning. Turn quilt. Slipstitch opening closed.

8. Referring to Machine Quilting, page 150, machine-quilt in-the-ditch along sashing strips and squares. Machine-quilt around hearts.

9. Cut notches in ends of ribbons and tie into bows. Tack a contrasting bow to center of each heart.

Animal Pal Bibs

Not only are these cute-as-a-button terry cloth bibs great for everyday use, but they also have a special touch that makes them real bazaar best-sellers. These animal pals have ears that can be removed to serve as washcloths! Now that's a practical idea that any parent will appreciate. You may either use purchased washcloths or finish the edges of lightweight terry cloth squares.

Animal Pal Bib

Fabrics and Materials (for 1 bib)

Patterns, pages 78 and 79
Tracing paper

White terry cloth	⅓ yard
Pastel fabric	8" square
Muslin	8" square
Solid color terry cloth	9" square

or

9" square washcloth
Tear-away stabilizer or white paper
Scraps for eyes and nose
Glue stick
Black, red, and threads to match face, eyes, and nose
1 package of ¼"-wide double-fold bias tape

Instructions

1. Using tracing paper and matching dots, trace complete bib base pattern. On wrong side of terry cloth, trace pattern and cut 2. Set aside.

2. Select puppy, bunny, or kitty face and trace correct seam line on wrong side of 8" cotton square. Turn fabric over and transfer placement for eyes, nose and mouth.

Place face wrong side up on 8" muslin square. Stitch on traced seam line, leaving an opening for turning at bottom of chin. Adding ¼" seam allowance, cut out face. Clip curves and turn. Turn under raw edges of opening and press face.

3. Referring to face pattern and photo for colors, trace eyes and nose on fabric scraps and cut out. Position pieces on face and adhere with glue stick.

Referring to Machine Appliqué, page 143, place stabilizer behind face. Using matching thread, machine-appliqué eyes and nose. Using red for mouth and black for whiskers, satin-stitch along traced lines. Remove stabilizer.

4. Using a scant ¼" seam, machine-baste bib front to back. Referring to photograph for placement, position bottom of face ¼" from edge of bib bottom and pin. Referring to face pattern, place pins at notches for ear openings.

5. For ears, use 9" square washcloth. If using 9" terry cloth square, round off corners; zigzag or serge edges. Referring to Diagram A, fold in corners of washcloth as shown in Figure 1. Then fold folded edges together. (See Figure 2.) Slide washcloth through ear openings, adjusting placement of pins if necessary. Remove washcloth.

Diagram A: Folding Washcloth
Figure 1

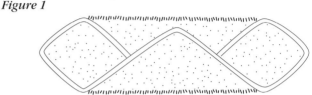

Figure 2

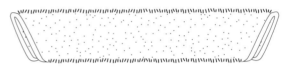

6. Using thread to match face, machine-appliqué around face, leaving openings for ears unstitched. Reverse stitching at ear openings to reinforce stitching.

7. Cut 32" of double-fold bias tape. Starting at corner of neck opening, bind outside edges of bib.

Cut 34" of bias tape and center tape on neckline. To make ties and bind neckline, begin at 1 end of bias tape and stitch long edges together; bind raw edge of neckline in stitching, and continue stitching to end of tie. Knot each end of tie.

8. For ears, re-fold washcloth as shown in Diagram A. For bunny, referring to Diagram B, pull folded washcloth through openings and pull ears up.

For puppy, referring to Diagram C, pull folded washcloth through openings and fold each side down. Press to hold shape.

For kitty, placing double-folded edge at top, pull through ear openings. Referring to Diagram D, fold ends under to form triangles and tuck in ear openings. Press to hold shape.

Diagram B: Bunny's Ears   **Diagram C: Puppy's Ears**    **Diagram D: Kitty's Ears**

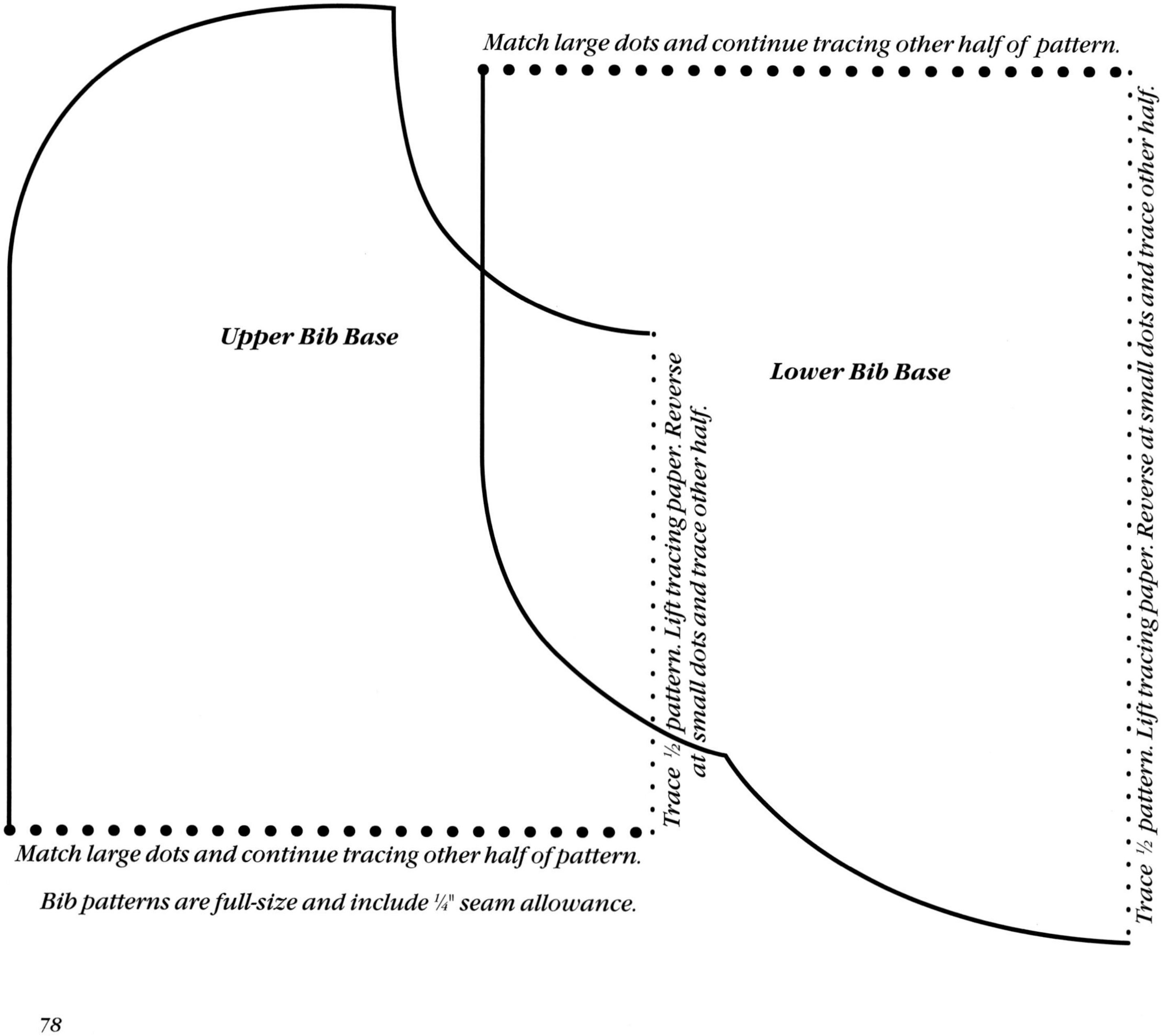

Match large dots and continue tracing other half of pattern.

Upper Bib Base

Lower Bib Base

Trace ½ pattern. Lift tracing paper. Reverse at small dots and trace other half.

Trace ½ pattern. Lift tracing paper. Reverse at small dots and trace other half.

Match large dots and continue tracing other half of pattern.

Bib patterns are full-size and include ¼" seam allowance.

Animal Pal Face
Pattern is full-size.
Add ¼" seam allowance
when cutting out face.

Trace pink line for bunny.

Trace orange line for puppy.

Trace blue line for kitty.

*Trace black eyes for bunny and puppy.
**Trace blue eyes for kitty.

Christmas Cornucopia

Your Christmas booth is guaranteed to attract a crowd at any time of the year. You'll want to make a multitude of little angels in calico. A peppermint-striped Calico Cat adds to the fun. Decorate the Country Patchwork Stocking with speedy appliqué shapes cut with pinking shears and finished with a colorful running stitch. And the golden stars are made just as quickly, with pinked edges adding to their charm. You'll find lots of stockings, ornaments, tree skirts, and more!

Lollipops and Candy Canes

In Sherwood, Arkansas, Pamela Houk was inspired by a bright fabric that suggested candy canes. She designed the easy hostess apron with a bright bib decorated with old-fashioned yo-yos. Swirls of red and white make delicious-looking lollipop ornaments, and the candy cane striped stocking has a wreath made of yo-yos. Jingle bells in the center of each one make this stocking a real favorite with children.

Lollipop Ornaments

Fabrics and Materials (for 1 ornament)

Red-and-white stripe	6½" square
Polyester stuffing	
5" (3/16"-diameter) wooden dowel	
White glue	
5/8"-wide red satin ribbon	½ yard
Red thread	

Instructions

1. Using pattern on page 157, make a 6" circle template. Trace circle on right side of fabric. Adding ¼" seam allowance, cut out circle.

Referring to Yo-Yos, page 145, turn under seam allowance while taking small running stitches through both layers. Place small amount of stuffing in center and pull thread tightly to gather yo-yo and enclose stuffing. Knot thread to secure. Distribute gathers and lightly press.

2. Clip a 3/16" opening in folded edge of yo-yo. Apply white glue to end of dowel and insert it 1" into clipped opening.

3. Cut 10" of ribbon and tie in a bow around dowel under yo-yo. For hanger loop, cut 7" of ribbon. Fold in half and tack ends to top back of ornament.

Holiday Hostess Apron

Fabrics and Materials

Red-and-white stripe	11" square
White batiste	1 yard
White eyelet edging fabric	1¼ yards
Green Christmas print	¼ yard
1"-wide pre-gathered white eyelet lace	1 yard
5/8"-wide red satin ribbon	½ yard
10 (3/8") red wooden beads	
Thread to match fabrics	

Pieces to Cut

5½" x 27½" strip	2 batiste
3" x 15¼" strip	2 batiste
3" x 30½" strip	4 batiste
36" x 22" rectangle*	1 eyelet
7" square	1 eyelet
3½" circle	10 green print

**Note*: Cut with eyelet border on 1 (36"-long) edge.

Instructions

1. To make apron bib: With stripes on 11" square running vertically, turn under ¼" twice on side and top edges. Press. With right sides up, pin bound edge of lace to wrong side of hem around sides and top of bib. Set aside.

2. For neck ties, with right sides facing and raw edges aligned, fold 1 (5½" x 27½") strip in half lengthwise. Stitch along long edge and 1 end. Clip corner, turn, and press. Turn under raw edges ¼" and press. Repeat for remaining tie.

Place open end of 1 tie on wrong side of 1 corner of bib, aligning end of tie with hem. Pin. Repeat for remaining tie. Topstitch along hem, catching edges of lace and ends of ties in stitching.

3. To make skirt: On eyelet rectangle, turn under ¼" twice on each side edge. Topstitch and press.

For pocket, on 7" eyelet square, with edging at top, turn under ¼" twice on sides and bottom. Measuring 6" down from top and 6" over from side of skirt, pin pocket in place.

Run a gathering thread along top edge of skirt and pull to gather to 14¾". Set aside.

4. To make waistband and ties, with right sides facing and raw ends aligned, join 1 (3" x 30½") tie to each end of 1 (3" x 15¼") waistband. Repeat to make a second strip. Press seams toward ties.

With right sides facing and raw edges aligned, pin waistband/tie strips together. On wrong side, mark center of each long raw edge. (See Diagram.) On 1 long edge, measure 5¾" on each side of center and mark (11½" total). On opposite long edge, measure 7⅜" on each side of center and mark (14¾" total). Stitch strips together, leaving openings in marked center spaces of waistband. Turn.

Turn raw edges under ¼" along both openings and press.

Waistband Piecing

5. Insert bottom raw edge of bib ¼" inside 11½" waistband opening and baste. Insert top gathered edge of skirt in remaining opening in same manner, adjusting gathers if necessary. Edgestitch waistband and ties through all layers, catching edges of bib and skirt in seam.

6. Referring to Yo-Yos, page 145, and making 3½" circle template from patterns on page 157, make 10 green print yo-yos.

Referring to photo for placement, pin yo-yos in Christmas tree shape on apron bib. Stitching through all layers, tack 1 bead in center of each yo-yo. Tie ribbon in a bow and tack under tree.

Yo-Yo Stocking

Fabrics and Materials
Tracing paper
Red-and-white stripe   ½ yard
Red (for lining)   ½ yard
Green Christmas print   ⅛ yard
Thin batting
8" (1"-wide) pre-gathered white eyelet lace
20" (⅝"-wide) red satin ribbon
7" (⅜"-wide) red satin ribbon
8 small jingle bells

Instructions
1. Using tracing paper, enlarge pattern, omitting toe and heel markings. Trace pattern onto striped fabric with stripes running lengthwise and cut 1 for stocking front. Reverse and cut 1 more for stocking back. Repeat for batting and lining, cutting lining on crossgrain.

2. Pin 1 batting piece each to wrong side of stocking front and back. With right sides facing and raw edges aligned, stitch stocking front to back, leaving top open. Repeat for lining. Remove pins. Clip curves and trim seams on stocking and lining. Turn stocking and press. Do not turn lining. On top raw edge of lining, fold down ¼" and press.

3. With wrong sides facing, slip lining inside stocking, aligning side seams. To make cuff: Fold lining 2¼" down over top edge of stocking. Starting at back of stocking, 1" away from back side seam, tuck bound edge of lace under folded hem of lining. Using thread to match lining, slipstitch lace to folded hem. Stop stitching 1" away from end of lace strip. Fold raw end of lace under ½", tuck under folded hem and complete slipstitching.

4. Referring to Yo-Yos, page 145, and making 3½" circle template from patterns on page 157, make 8 green print yo-yos. Arrange yo-yos on stocking front as shown in photo and pin. Stitching through front layers only, tack 1 bell in center of each yo-yo and remove pin. Tie ⅜"-wide ribbon in a bow and tack under wreath.

For hanger loop, fold ⅜"-wide ribbon in half and tack ends to inside stocking at right seam.

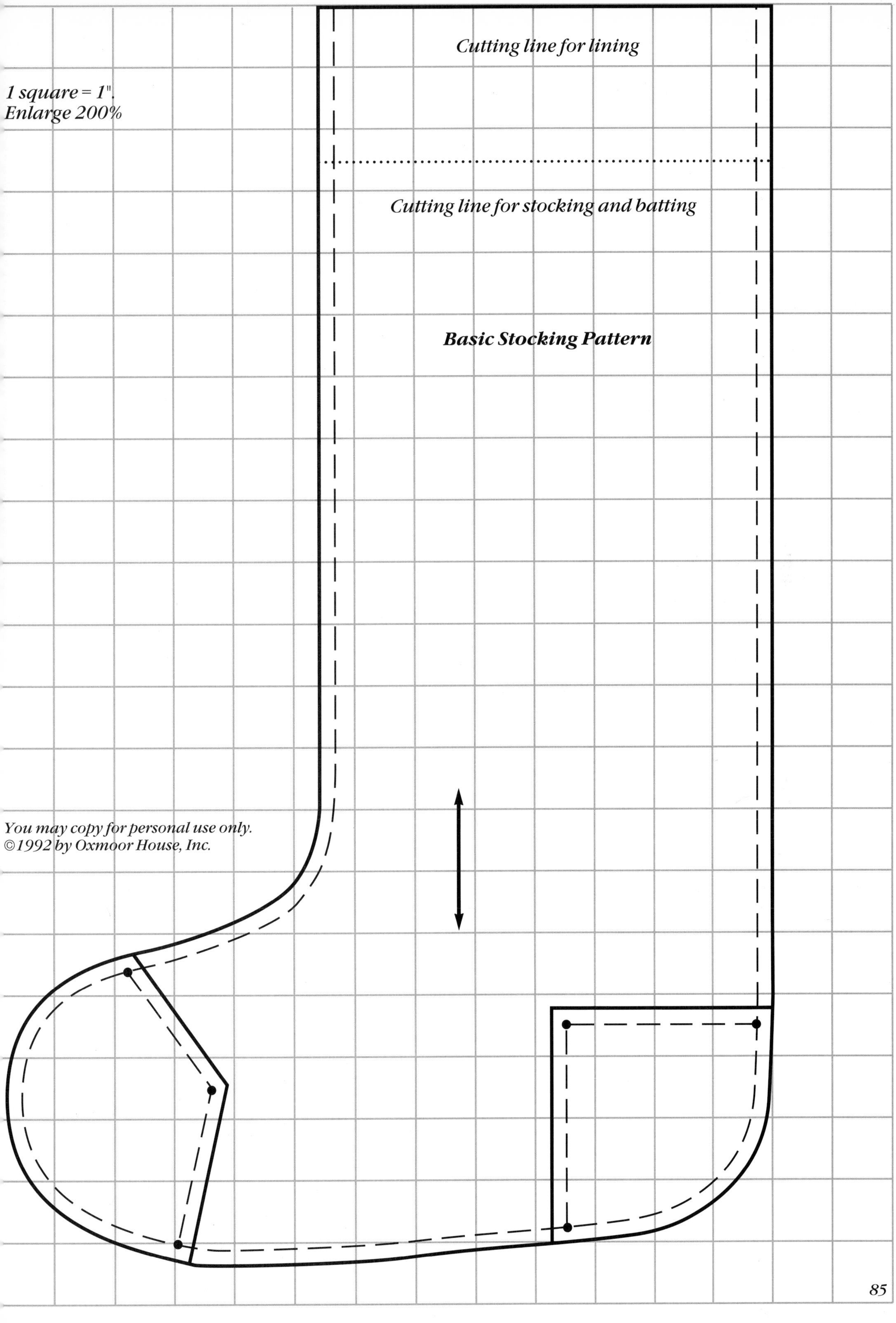

1 square = 1".
Enlarge 200%

Cutting line for lining

Cutting line for stocking and batting

Basic Stocking Pattern

You may copy for personal use only.
©1992 by Oxmoor House, Inc.

Candy Cane Party Mats

Wrapped in red-and-white candy cane spirals, these party mats designed by Marilyn Dorwart, of Delray Beach, Florida, are great for holiday entertaining. With handy pockets to hold utensils and a napkin, these are smart accessories for the buffet table or a family supper by the Christmas tree. When they're unrolled, the mats can be spread with the striped side up across the lap or on a tray table for neater dining.

Fabrics and Materials (for set of 4)*

Red fabric	1 yard
White fabric	½ yard
Lt. Christmas print (for lining)	1 yard
Green Christmas print (for napkin)	⅞ yard
Batting	
Red (for binding)	½ yard

or

2 packages of ¼"-wide double-fold red bias tape

⅜"-wide green grosgrain ribbon	4 yards

Threads to match fabrics

Pieces to Cut

14" x 18" rectangle	4 lining
	4 batting
11" x 13" rectangle	4 red
2½" x 45" strip	8 red
1" x 44" crosswise strip	6 red
	6 white
1½" x 44" strip	6 white
4"-long piece	4 green ribbon
12½"-long piece	4 green ribbon
15" square	4 green print

▶▶▶ **TIME-SAVER**

*Instead of string piecing, you can use striped fabric to make the mats. You'll need 1¼ yards of fabric for striped sides of 4 mats. For each, with stripes at a 45° angle, cut 1 (12½" x 16½") rectangle. Cut 1 print lining and 1 batting rectangle the same size as front. Layer lining (right side down), batting, and striped rectangle (right side up) and pin. Machine-quilt along printed stripes at about 3" intervals. Then begin with Step 4 to complete the mat.

Instructions

1. For each mat, place 1 batting on wrong side of 1 lining. Leaving 6" square at bottom left corner free, pin all around.

2. Referring to Diagram, Figure 1, lay 1 (2½") red strip, right side up, diagonally across bottom left corner. Trim excess length of red strip. With right sides facing and top raw edges aligned, lay 1 (1½") white strip on top of red, trimming excess white strip. Stitch through all layers, as shown in Figure 2. Flip white strip back and press, removing any pins in this area. Repeat, adding more strips in this order: 1" red, 1" white, 2½" red. Continue to add strips in this sequence until rectangle is covered.

3. Turn mat over. Trim mat to 12½" x 16½".

4. To make utensil pocket: Fold 11" x 13" rectangle in quarters to measure 5½" x 6½". With lining side of mat up and 5½"-long fold at top, align raw edges of pocket with raw edges of bottom left corner of mat. Pin. Make napkin holder by tucking raw end of 4" piece of ribbon ¼" under upper right edge of pock-

String Piecing
Figure 1

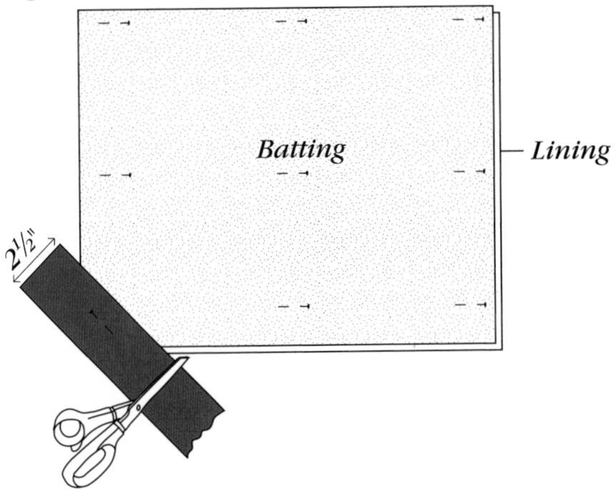

Figure 2

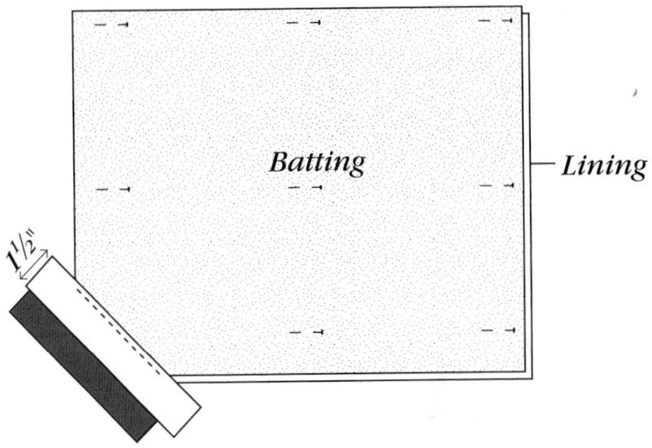

et. Edgestitch pocket on 3 sides, leaving top open and catching end of ribbon in stitching. Straighten ribbon horizontally, turn other end of ribbon under ¼", and stitch end to lining (see photo).

For utensil pocket divisions, draw a vertical line 1¾" from left edge of pocket. Draw a second line 1¾" from first. Topstitch on marked lines.

5. Using a small plate or French curve as a guide, round off corners on mat.

6. For tie, fold 1 (12½") green ribbon in half to find center. On striped side of mat, on opposite edge from pocket, center ribbon vertically, aligning folded edge of ribbon with raw edge of mat. Pin.

7. For binding, piece 1"-wide bias strips of red fabric to total 55", or cut a 55" length of double-fold bias tape. Bind raw edges, catching folded ribbon in seam. Repeat to make remaining mats.

8. To make napkins: On each 15" green square, either serge edges or turn under ¼" twice on all edges and topstitch hem.

★ **BAZAAR TIP**
Feature this project in other booths at your bazaar as well. In bright colors, these party mats will make neat accessories for picnics or barbecues. Make sets of red, white, and blue party mats for a Fourth of July celebration, or use vivid tropical prints with coordinating solids to enjoy all summer long.

Music Box Ornaments

Within each of these patchwork ornaments, there's a secret that makes them irresistible. Tiny musical disks that play Christmas carols are sewn inside each ornament. Everyone loves to squeeze them to hear the music play! The music boxes are very inexpensive, and they're available at most craft stores. You'll find that adding this extra touch really pays off.

Star and Square Ornament

Fabrics and Materials
Patterns, page 152
Scraps of red print, red solid fabric
Red thread
Scrap of batting
1⅜ " music box disk
8" (¼"-wide) red ribbon
Ornament hook

Pieces to Cut
Template S2	2 red print
Template T1	8 red solid
2" x 4" rectangle	1 batting

Instructions

1. With right sides facing and raw edges aligned, fold T1s in half along long edge. Stitch as shown in Diagram, Figure 1. Clip corners, trim seams, and turn.
2. Place S2 right side up. Referring to Figure 2, pin open ends of 2 T1s to 1 side of S2. Stitch from corner dot to corner dot. Repeat to join pairs of triangles to remaining sides of S2.

Making Star
Figure 1   Figure 2

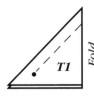
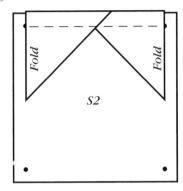

3. With right sides facing and raw edges aligned, pin second S2 over assembled unit and stitch around 3 sides, catching ends of triangles in seam and leaving an opening for turning. Clip corners and turn.
4. Fold batting in half to make a 2" square. Insert music box disk between batting layers and baste around disk to secure.
5. Stuff batting and music box into opening in star. Slipstitch opening closed.
6. Referring to photo for placement, tie ribbon into a bow and tack to star front. Tack ornament hook to back.

Star Poinsettia Ornament

Fabrics and Materials
Pattern, page 153
Red solid fabric or red print 9" square
Scrap of yellow fabric
Scraps of batting or polyester stuffing
Thread to match fabrics
1⅜" music box disk
Ornament hook

Pieces to Cut
Template B2   12 red

Instructions

1. Referring to Flower Basket block, Step 1, page 12, join 6 B2s to make 1 (6-pointed) star for ornament front. Repeat to join remaining 6 B2s to make second star for ornament back, leaving 1½" opening in center seam between halves.

2. With right sides facing and raw edges aligned, pin front to back and stitch around outside edges to join. Trim and turn through opening in center back seam.
3. Partially stuff with batting, tuck music box disk in center, and complete stuffing. Slipstitch opening closed.
4. Referring to Yo-Yos, page 145, and making 2½" circle template from pattern on page 157, make 1 yellow yo-yo. Tack to center of ornament front.
5. Tack ornament hook to back.

Tulip Ornament

Fabrics and Materials
Patterns, pages 90 and 157
Scraps of red pindot, green print, white print
Thread to match fabrics
Freezer paper (for hand appliqué)
or
Paper-backed fusible web*
Polyester stuffing
Batting
White quilting thread (optional)
1⅜" music box disk
8" (¼"-wide) red ribbon
Ornament hook

Pieces to cut
5" circle   2 white print
                                   2 batting

Instructions

1. For hand appliqué, trace all pattern pieces, page 90, on dull side of freezer paper. Referring to Freezer Paper Hand Appliqué, page 143, prepare appliqué pieces: 1 green print stem, 2 green print leaves, 1 red pindot petal A, 1 red print petal B, and 1 red pindot petal C.
   On right side of 1 (5") circle, appliqué pieces in this order: stem, leaves, petals A, B, and C.

▶▶▶ **TIME-SAVER**

*For your bazaar, you'll have time to make many more of these pretty tulip ornaments when you fuse the appliqués in place. Refer to Paper-backed Fusible Web, page 143.

To make multiples, cut several 5" circles and fuse all of the appliqués before beginning to assemble the ornaments.

2. Pin 1 circle of batting to wrong side of appliquéd piece. If desired, quilt around flower, stem, and leaves ⅛" from edges of appliqué.
3. Center music box disk on batting side of appliquéd piece. Pin second batting circle over

music box. Baste around disk through batting layers only to secure disk.

4. With right sides facing and raw edges aligned, stitch backing circle to appliquéd piece, leaving a 3" opening at bottom for turning. Clip curves, trim seam, and turn. Add extra stuffing. Slipstitch opening closed.

5. Referring to photo for placement, tie ribbon into a bow and tack bow and ornament hook to top as shown.

Tulip Pattern

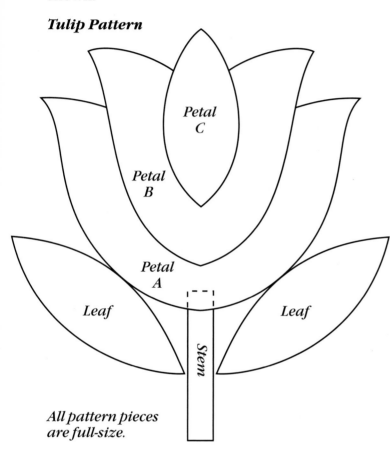

All pattern pieces are full-size.

BAZAAR TIP

You can add more fun and extra income for your bazaar by including a booth selling photos with Santa. You'll need some enthusiastic volunteers, a Santa costume, and someone who is skilled with the use of a Polaroid camera. You'll also need to set up a decorated area for Santa's visits and folders to hold the photos.

These arrangements require planning by a special committee, but it could be worth the extra effort. Many holiday bazaars are finding this a popular and very profitable feature.

Charming Calico Ornaments

The Calico Cat, Christmas Bear, and Calico Angels were designed by Sue von Jentzen, from Granite Falls, Washington. Make some of each so that bazaargoers can choose their favorites. You'll probably find enough pieces in your scrap bag to make a collection of these charmers.

Calico Angel

Fabrics and Materials (for 1 angel)
Patterns, page 93
Dk. print   8" square
Lt. print   4" x 8" rectangle
Scrap of muslin
Polyester stuffing
Embroidery floss: red, black, gold
Threads to match fabrics
4" (⅛"-wide) ribbon
2 beads, jingle bells, or buttons
7" piece of crochet cotton
3 yards of yarn for hair (optional)
2½" square of cardboard (optional)

Instructions
1. With right sides facing, fold 8" dark print square in half and pin. Trace pattern for dress on wrong side of folded fabric. Set aside.

With right sides facing, fold light print rectangle in half widthwise and pin. Trace pattern for wings on wrong side of folded fabric. Set aside.

From muslin, cut 1 (3½" x 6") rectangle. Fold muslin in half widthwise and pin. Trace pattern for body on folded fabric.

2. To make body: Stitch muslin along traced line, leaving bottom open. Adding ⅛" seam allowance, cut out. Clip curves, turn, and stuff firmly. Slipstitch bottom closed.

3. Referring to Embroidery Stitches, page 145, embroider face as follows:* Using 3 strands of floss, make black French knots for eyes and 1 red straightstitch for mouth.

▶▶▶ **TIME-SAVER**
*You can make facial features much more quick-
ly by using red and black permanent marking
pens to make dots for the eyes and a straight line
for the mouth.

To make hair: Using 6 strands gold floss, make 8
French knots. (For optional yarn hair: Wind yarn
around cardboard 15–20 times. Slip loops off cardboard. Wrap a short piece of yarn around center
and tie in a knot. Tie a small piece of yarn ¼" from
each folded end. Tack hair to head at top and
sides.)

4. To make dress: Stitch along traced line, leaving
openings at neck and sleeves as indicated on pattern. Adding ⅛" seam allowance, cut out. Clip corners and turn.

5. To make hands: From muslin, cut 1¼" x 3¼" strip.
Fold strip in half lengthwise. Aligning raw edges,
stitch long edges together. Turn. Tie 1 bead, bell, or
button to each end of ribbon. Referring to Diagram,
page 92, and placing ribbon in center of muslin, tie
hand piece in a single knot.

6. To make wings: With right sides facing and raw
edges aligned, stitch along traced line. Adding ⅛"
seam allowance, cut out. Cut a slit through *top layer*
only. Clip curves and turn through slit. Slipstitch
opening closed. Edgestitch if desired.

Making Hands

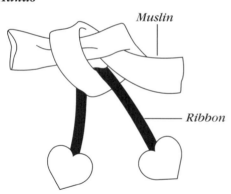

Muslin

Ribbon

7. To assemble dress: Fold neck edge under ⅛". With matching thread, run a gathering thread around neck opening. Leave needle threaded. Insert body into dress and pull to gather dress around neck. Using threaded needle, tack dress to body.

Gather each sleeve in same manner and fold to center front of dress. Insert 1 end of hand piece into each sleeve and tack hands to sleeves.

With slit facing back of dress, tack top center of wings to dress about ¼" from neck.

For hanger loop, stitch crochet cotton through top back of head. Knot ends together.

Hint: For a pretty touch, put a little powdered blush on a cotton swab and rub on a paper towel to remove excess. Lightly rouge angel's cheeks.

Calico Cat and Christmas Bear Ornament

Fabrics and Materials (for 1 ornament)

Print fabric	4" x 8" rectangle
⅛"-wide ribbon (for cat)	¼ yard
⅛"-wide ribbon (for bear)	⅓ yard
Polyester stuffing	
Thread to match	
Needle	
Metallic cord	

Instructions

1. With right sides facing and raw edges aligned, fold fabric in half to make a 4" square. Trace pattern on wrong side of folded fabric.

2. Machine-stitch on traced line, leaving an opening for turning. Adding ⅛" seam allowance, cut out. Clip curves and turn.

3. Stuff firmly. Slipstitch opening closed.

Note: For bear, referring to pattern for placement, make small running stitches by hand through top layer of fabric only. Pull to gather stitches slightly and knot to secure.

4. Tie ribbon in bow at neck and tack to secure. Trim ends.

5. For hanger loop, stitch metallic cord through top back of head. Knot ends together.

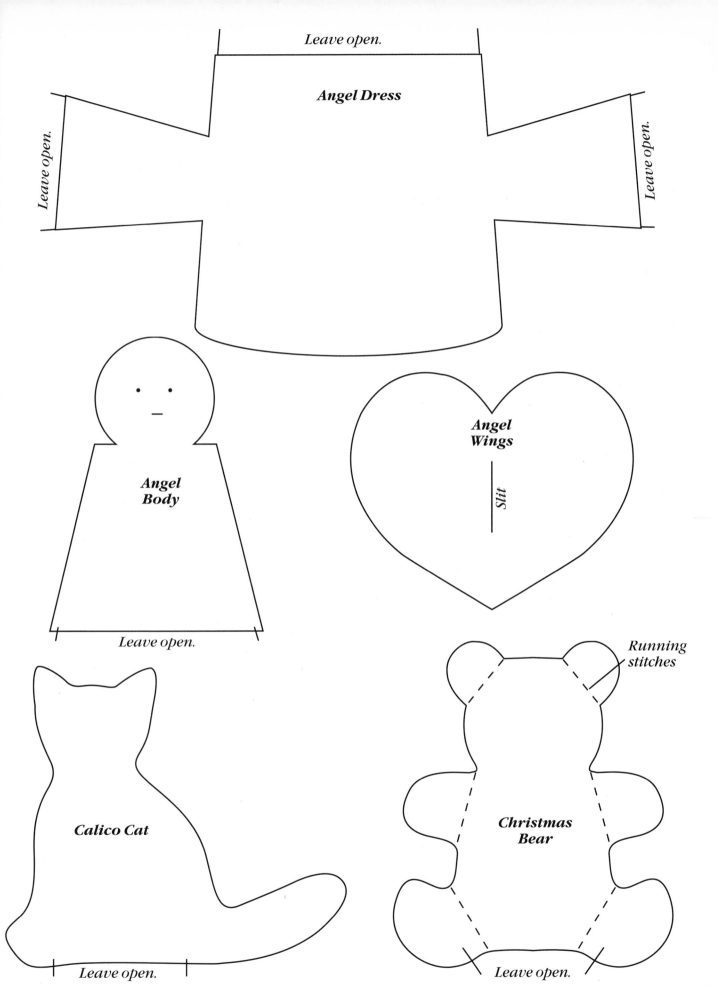

Leave open.

Angel Dress

Leave open.

Leave open.

**Angel
Body**

**Angel
Wings**

Slit

Leave open.

Calico Cat

Running
stitches

**Christmas
Bear**

Leave open.

Leave open.

in record time, instructions are given for cutting all of the pieces without patterns; squares are cut to make half-square or quarter-square triangles with correct grain lines. Whether you cut the pieces with a rotary cutter or with scissors, it's one of the fastest and prettiest patchwork tree skirts ever!

Hearts and Flowers Stocking

Fabrics and Materials

Patterns, pages 85 and 97	
Basic stenciling supplies listed on page 143	
Fabric paint: red, green	
Masking tape	
White-on-white print	½ yard
Red print (for lining)	½ yard
Batting	
White quilting thread (optional)	
Gold-and-white twisted braid	⅔ yard
⅝"-wide gold metallic ribbon	1 yard
Thread to match fabrics	

Instructions

1. Referring to Yo-Yo stocking, Step 1, page 84, enlarge and trace stocking pattern, including heel and toe. Cut out stocking, lining, and batting. Trace lines for heel and toe on right side of stocking front.
2. Referring to Stenciling, page 143, and using Hearts and Flowers Pattern on page 97, prepare stencils to be done with red: hearts and tulip petals. Make a stencil for green: tulip base and stem. Place masking tape along traced lines for heel and toe to create areas to be painted in red. Referring to photo for placement, apply paint to all red areas on stocking and let dry thoroughly. Stencil green areas. Let dry.

Pin batting to wrong side of stocking front. Quilt around stenciled designs by hand or machine, if desired.
3. Referring to Yo-Yo Stocking, Steps 2 and 3, page 84, assemble stocking. After folding lining down over top of stocking to make cuff, starting on back of stocking, slipstitch braid to folded edge of lining. At end of stitching, clip braid, tuck raw ends under cuff, and stitch in place.
4. For hanger loop, cut 8" of braid and fold in half. Tack ends inside stocking at right seam. Tie gold ribbon in bow and tack to stocking at bottom of cuff.

Holiday Hearts and Flowers

Beautiful stenciling really has a chance to shine when it's applied to a white-on-white print, as in the elegant stocking and tree skirt shown here. When the paint is added, the design pops out, just as if it were appliquéd. Quilting by hand or machine around the stenciled designs is optional, but it will enhance this effect.

The Christmas tree skirt is really a giant Ohio Star block. So that you can make it

Hearts and Flowers Tree Skirt

Fabrics and Materials

Patterns, pages 96 and 97
Basic stenciling supplies listed on page 143
Fabric paint: red, green

Green print	⅓ yard
Red print	⅔ yard
White-on-white print	1 yard
Backing	1¼ yards
Batting	44" square

2 packages of ½"-wide double-fold bias tape
Thread to match fabrics

Pieces to Cut

22¼" square	1 white print

(Cut in *quarters* diagonally for 4 As.)

16⅛" square	1 white print

(Cut in *quarters* diagonally for 4 Bs.)

11⅜" square	4 red print
	2 green print

(Cut each in *half* diagonally for 8 red Cs and 4 green Ds.

6⅛" square	1 white print
	2 red print

(Cut each in *quarters* diagonally, for 4 white Es and 8 red Fs.)

5⅜" square (G)	4 white print
7½" square (H)	1 green print

Tree Skirt Assembly

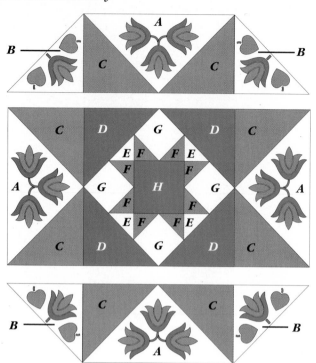

Instructions

1. Referring to Stenciling, page 143, prepare stencils for each color, using patterns given here. Working with 1 color at a time, stencil Tulips design on 4 triangle As and Hearts and Flowers design on 4 triangle Bs. Let dry. Heat-set with a dry iron.

2. Referring to Diagram and photo for color placement, join pieces as shown.

3. Stack backing (right side down), batting, and tree skirt top (right side up). Referring to Basting With Safety Pins, page 148, pin-baste. Trim excess batting and backing.

Referring to Machine Quilting, page 150, machine-quilt in-the-ditch along all seam lines. Quilt around stenciled designs, if desired. Remove pins.

4. Using 6" circle pattern on page 157, trace circle in center of H. Referring to photo, draw a straight line from circle to outside edge of 1 triangle A. Stitching ¼" from drawn lines, topstitch from outside edge to circle, continue stitching around circle, and then stitch on opposite side of drawn line to outside edge.

Cut on drawn line between lines of stitching. Leaving a ¼" seam allowance, cut out center circle.

5. Bind cut straight edges and center circle. Bind outer edges of tree skirt.

Tulip Stencil Pattern
Pattern is full-size.

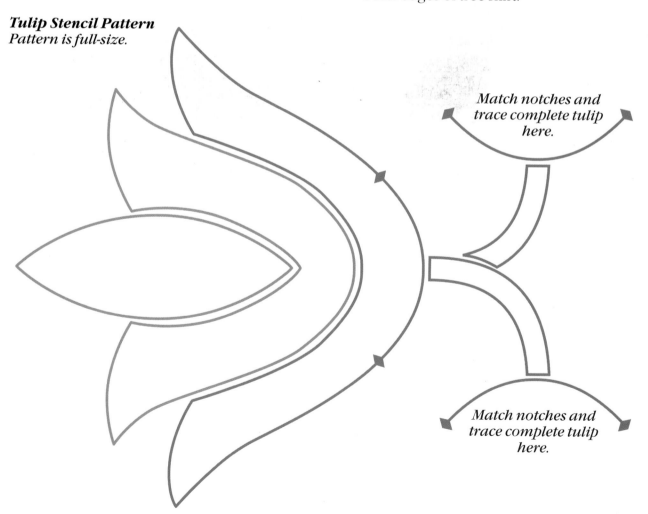

Match notches and trace complete tulip here.

Match notches and trace complete tulip here.

Hearts and Flowers Stencil Pattern
Pattern is full-size.

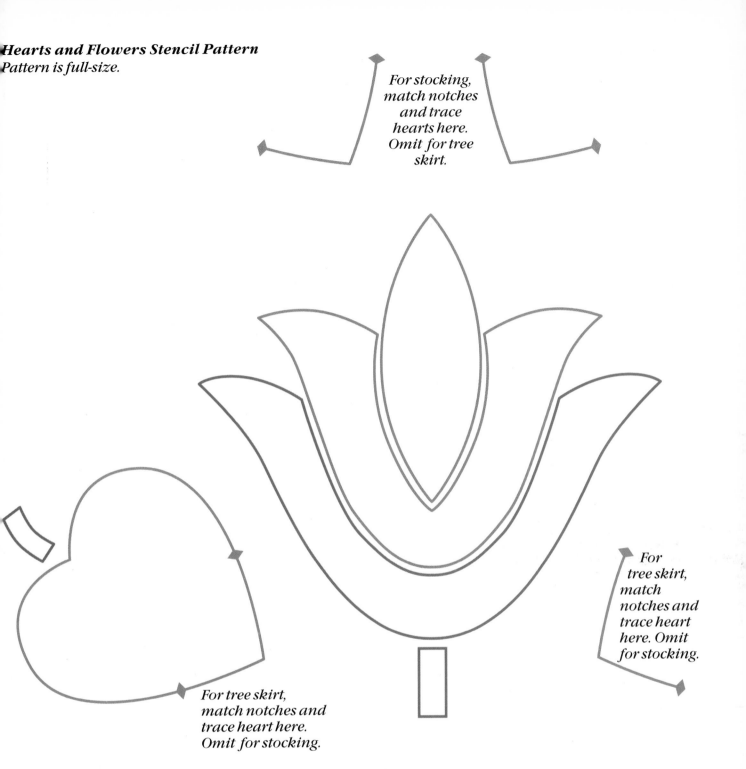

For stocking, match notches and trace hearts here. Omit for tree skirt.

For tree skirt, match notches and trace heart here. Omit for stocking.

For tree skirt, match notches and trace heart here. Omit for stocking.

Country Christmas Calicoes

Warm prints and checks create homey holiday decorations with a country flavor. The easy garland of stars on the grapevine wreath could also glow against an evergreen wreath, or they might be used as a mantel swag. Brightly colored running stitches accent the soft gold stars on the wreath and light up the country prints on the Christmas stocking.

You can make bushels of red apples for garlands, ornaments, or package toppers with a speedy technique which will make a batch of easy multiples. And the calico patches on the red-and-green checkerboard tree skirt have an old-fashioned look, but they are joined in record time by using rotary cutting and strip piecing.

Star Garland Wreath

Fabrics and Materials
Patterns, page 156
Muslin .... ¼ yard
Assorted scraps of gold print
Polyester stuffing
Embroidery floss: red, green, blue
¼"-wide red satin ribbon .... 1½ yard
21 (⅜"-diameter) wooden beads
12"-diameter grapevine wreath

Pieces to Cut
6" square	3 muslin
	3 gold print
4 ½" square	3 muslin
	3 gold print

Instructions
1. Center and lightly trace Star #2 on right side of each 6" print square. Center and trace Star #1 on right side of each 4 ½" square.
2. With wrong sides facing and raw edges aligned, pin 1 print and 1 muslin same-size square together. Make 6 pairs.
3. Using 3 strands of red, green, or blue embroidery floss, take running stitches along traced line, stopping 1" from where stitching began. Leave needle threaded. Stuff star firmly, and then continue running stitches to complete line of stitching. Secure thread. Repeat for remaining stars.
4. Using pinking shears and adding ¼" seam allowance, cut out each star.
5. Thread 21 wooden beads on ribbon, tying knots at each end of ribbon to secure. Leaving 3 beads at 1 end, slide remaining beads toward other end. Measuring 8" from beaded end, tack back of large star to ribbon. Slide 3 beads back to edge of star. Close to third bead, tack a small star to ribbon. Repeat, placing 3 beads between stars and alternating large and small stars. Slide last 3 beads to end of ribbon.
6. Arrange Star Garland around wreath and tack to secure. Tie ends of ribbon in bow.

BAZAAR TIP
The quick method used to make these stars can be used to produce many ornaments for your bazaar. Any of the hearts, stars, or apple patterns, page 156, or tree patterns, page 157, may be used; just be sure that your fabric square is large enough to let you add the ¼" seam allowance when cutting out the shape with pinking shears.

Instead of using muslin for the ornament backs, you can use assorted prints from your scrap bag for both sides of the ornaments. The prints for the fronts and backs don't have to match. That's part of their country charm!

Choose a bright contrasting color of embroidery floss for the running stitches. Assemble the ornaments following Steps 1–4 above. Then add a hanger loop made from the same color of floss at the top of each ornament.

A variety of prints, shapes, and colors will make an eye-catching display! Your bazaar can have plenty of these ornaments because they take so little time to make.

Enlarge and tranfer 1 heel and 1 toe pattern to scraps of lining fabric. Cut outer curved lines with regular scissors. Cut straight inside lines with pinking shears.

For hanger loop, cut a 1" x 7" strip from scrap of lining fabric with pinking shears.

Using tree patterns, page 157, trace 1 of each size on green print. Using Star #2 pattern, page 156, trace 1 star on gold print. With pinking shears, cut out all shapes just inside marked lines.

2. With right sides up and raw edges aligned, position heel and toe pieces on stocking front and pin. Using 3 strands of green floss, use running stitches ¼" from pinked edges to stitch pieces to stocking. Referring to photo for placement, pin trees in place. Using red floss, appliqué in same manner. At center bottom of each tree, make chainstitches for trunk as shown in photo. (See Embroidery Stitches, page 145.)

3. Referring to Yo-Yo Stocking, Steps 2 and 3, page 84, assemble stocking. Instead of turning under top edge of lining, use pinking shears to trim.

To make cuff: Turn lining 2¼" down over top edge of stocking and press. Position star as shown in photo, overlapping edge of cuff ½". With red floss, appliqué in same manner as trees, stitching through stocking front and lining layers. With green floss, make running stitches completely around cuff ¼" away from pinked edge.

4. Fold hanger loop in half and tack ends inside stocking at right seam. If desired, tack gold stars to front of stocking with 1 seed bead in center of each star.

Country Patchwork Stocking

Fabrics and Materials
Patterns, pages 85, 156, and 157
Dk. print — ½ yard
Check or plaid (for lining) — ½ yard
Thin batting
Scraps of gold prints, green prints
Pinking shears
Embroidery floss: red, green
6-8 (⅝") gold sequin stars (optional)
6-8 gold seed beads (optional)

Instructions
1. Referring to Yo-Yo Stocking, Step 1, page 84, trace and cut out pieces for stocking, lining, and batting.

Apple Garland

Fabrics and Materials (for 2 garlands)
Pattern, page 156
Red print — ¼ yard
Red solid fabric — ¼ yard
Thread to match fabrics
Seam ripper
Polyester stuffing
½"-wide green picot satin ribbon — 2¼ yards
⅛"-wide green satin ribbon — 2¼ yards

Pieces to Cut
2½" x 22½" crosswise strip	2 red print (backing)
	2 red solid (backing)
4½" x 22½" strip	1 red print
	1 red solid
8" pieces	10 (⅛"-wide) ribbon
40" pieces	2 (½"-wide) ribbon

100

Instructions

1. With right sides facing and raw edges aligned, machine-baste 2 (2½" x 22½") red print backing strips together along 1 long edge. Press seam open. Repeat for red solid strips. Set aside solid strip.

2. Make template of Apple #2 pattern. Referring to Diagram and leaving ½" between apples, trace 5 apples on wrong side of red print pieced-backing strip.

Pieced Backing

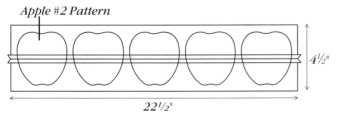

Apple #2 Pattern

4½"

22½"

3. With right sides facing and raw edges aligned, place marked backing strip on top of 4½" x 22½" red print strip. Pin. Machine-stitch completely around each apple along traced lines. Adding ¼ " seam allowance, cut out apples.

4. On center back of each apple, use seam ripper to remove 1" of machine-basting stitches to make opening for turning. Clip curves and turn. Stuff apples firmly. Using matching thread, slipstitch opening closed.

   Tie 1 (8") piece of ⅛"-wide green ribbon in a bow and tack ¼" down from center top of apple front. Repeat for remaining apples.

5. Using 4½" x 22½" red solid strip and solid pieced-backing strip, repeat Steps 2–4 to make 5 solid red apples.

6. To assemble garland: Starting 8" from end of 40" length of ½" green ribbon, alternating solid and print apples, tack 1 apple every 6". Repeat to make second garland from remaining apples.

Patchwork Tree Skirt

Fabrics and Materials

Green print	¾ yard
Red print	½ yard
White print	⅓ yard
Backing	1¼ yards
Batting	44" square

1 skein of red acrylic yarn (for tying)
Yarn needle
2 packages of ¼"-wide red double-fold bias tape

Pieces to Cut

4" x 45" crosswise strip	5 green print
	2 red print
	2 white print
4⅜" square	2 green print
	8 red print

Instructions

1. From green crosswise strips, cut 3 (32"-long) strips and 2 (16"-long) strips. From remainder of green strips, cut 21 (4") squares.

From red crosswise strips, cut 2 (32"-long) strips and 4 (4") squares.

From white crosswise strips, cut 3 (16"-long) strips and 8 (4") squares.

Cut 2 (4⅜") green squares in half diagonally to yield 4 green triangles. Then cut 8 (4⅜") squares in half diagonally to yield 16 red triangles.

2. Referring to Diagram A, join 32"-long green and red strips along long edges, alternating colors as shown. Cut across pieced band at 4" intervals.

Join 3 (16"-long) white and 2 (16"-long) green strips along long edges, alternating colors, and cut in same manner.

3. Referring to Diagram B, alternating green/red and white/green strips, assemble 4 checkerboard units. Set aside.

4. Join remaining squares and triangles as shown in Diagram C to make center unit and side units.

Join all units as shown.

5. Stack backing (right side down), batting, and tree skirt top (right side up). Referring to Basting with Safety Pins, page 148, pin-baste. Trim excess batting and backing. Thread needle with 2 (10") strands of yarn and sew through each layer in center of each white square. Tie yarn ends in a bow.

6. Referring to Hearts and Flowers Tree Skirt, Steps 4 and 5, page 96, cut opening and bind tree skirt.

Diagram A: Strip Piecing

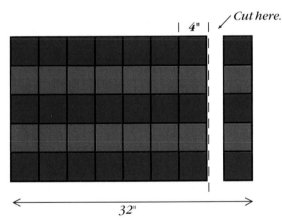

Diagram C: Tree Skirt Assembly

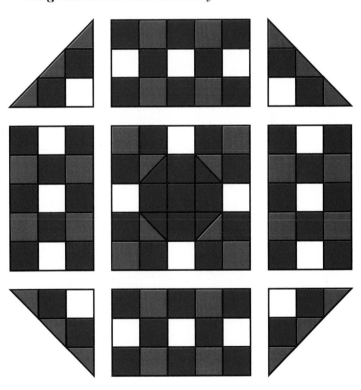

Diagram B: Checkerboard Unit

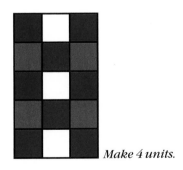

Make 4 units.

Gracious Gifts

The touch of the crafter's hands makes a very personal gift. You can see it in the old-fashioned Heart-and-Hand Needle Keeper. Here, too, fabric scraps become a beautiful Rose corsage and a cute Log Cabin Pincushion. There's also a Patchwork Belt and a Keepsake Heart Pin adorned with button flowers. With the addition of Seminole piecing, you can make bath towels into Shower Wraps. The elegant Folded Bags with their colorful borders are folded from quilt squares.

Ohio Star Wall Quilt

This wall quilt makes smart use of a beautiful border print that is repeated in a striped design across the fabric. The assembly method is a combination of strip piecing and template piecing that works together to assure that the triangles come together accurately, with all of the seam allowances included. Plan on cutting the borders after the center motif has been assembled, so that you can vary the border width depending on the printed design of your fabric. The fabric requirements include plenty for borders.

Finished Size
Wall quilt: 38" x 38"
Blocks: 9 (9" square)

Fabrics and Materials
Pattern, page 108	
Border print fabric	1½ yards*
Cream print	⅜ yard
Turquoise print	⅜ yard
Rose fabric	¼ yard
Muslin	1½ yards
Batting	
Thread to match fabrics	
Fabric for binding	¼ yard

or
2 packages of 1"-wide double-fold bias tape for binding
Note: Rows of border print should run parallel to selvages on fabric and have at least 6 design repeats.

Pieces to Cut
4" x 45" crosswise strip	2 cream print
3½" x 45" crosswise strip	1 border print
Template A	8 turquoise
	4 rose
	4 border print
Template B	4 cream print
Template C	4 border print

Instructions
1. To make corner units: Referring to Diagram A, Figure 1, join 2 cream print strips to 1 border print strip along long edges as shown. Press seams toward border print. Cut across pieced band as shown, making 4 (10½") squares.

Referring to Figure 2, cut squares in half diagonally exactly as shown, making 8 triangles. Trim ½"

from long cream print side of each triangle. (See Diagram B, Figure 1.)

Match pairs of triangles with diagonal cuts in opposite directions. (See Figure 2.) With right sides facing and raw edges aligned, join 1 pair of triangles along long edge. Press. Repeat to join 3 remaining pairs of triangles for corner units.
2. With right sides facing and raw edges aligned, join cream print Bs to border print Cs. Press seams toward border print.

To assemble Ohio Star unit: Join 1 B/C unit, 2 turquoise As, and 1 rose A as shown in Diagram C. Press. Repeat to make 3 more squares.

For center square, join 4 border print As.
3. Referring to photo for placement, join units to make center motif. Press.
4. To add mitered borders: Cut 4 (5½" x 41") strips from border print. *Hint: If you want to adjust the width of your quilt borders to suit the width of the design printed in your border fabric, first determine how wide you want the quilt border to be. Then, to find the length to cut, measure the length of the pieced center, plus twice the border width, plus 3" extra. Cut 4 strips this length.* Referring to Mitered Borders, page 147, join borders to center.
5. For backing, cut muslin same size as quilt top. Stack backing, batting, and quilt top (right side up). Using safety pins, pin layers together.
6. Referring to Machine Quilting, page 150, and Diagram D, machine-quilt in-the-ditch as shown.
7. Referring to Binding, page 150, apply straight-grain binding, using 2"-wide strips, or bind raw edges with bias tape.
8. Referring to Hanging Sleeve, page 151, add muslin sleeve to back of quilt.

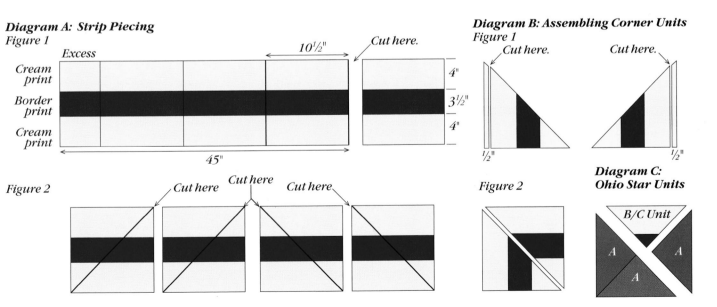

Diagram A: Strip Piecing
Figure 1

Diagram B: Assembling Corner Units
Figure 1

Diagram C: Ohio Star Units

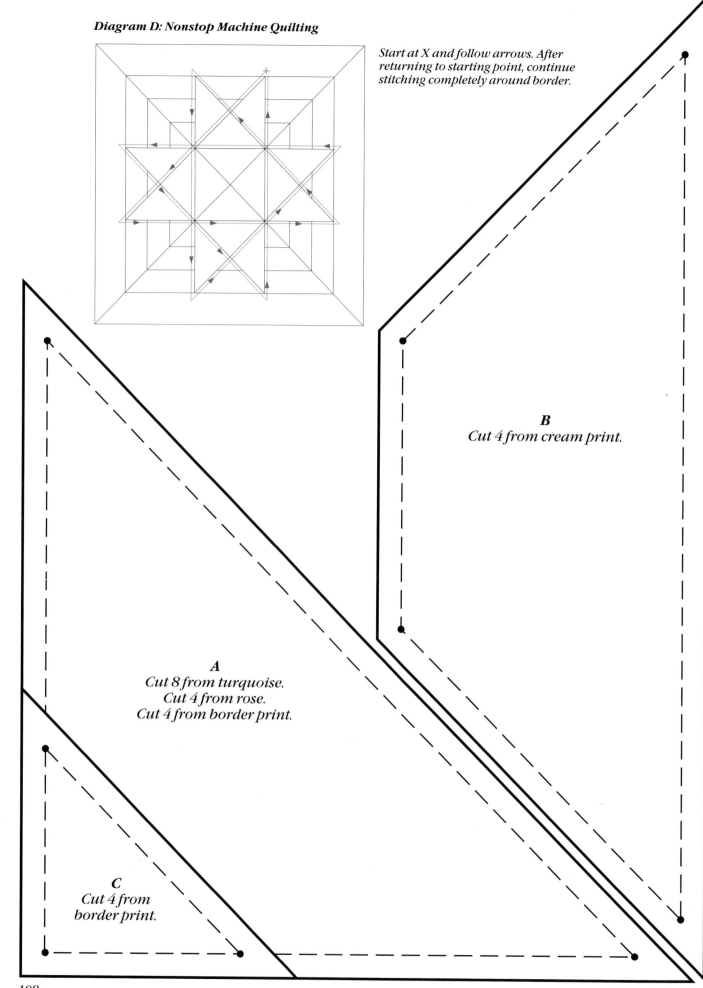

Diagram D: Nonstop Machine Quilting

Start at X and follow arrows. After returning to starting point, continue stitching completely around border.

B
Cut 4 from cream print.

A
Cut 8 from turquoise.
Cut 4 from rose.
Cut 4 from border print.

C
Cut 4 from border print.

Armchair Sewing Caddy

This handy caddy is ideal for those who like to keep their needlework close by. It's just the right size to drape over the arm of a comfortable chair by the fireside or on the front porch. There are two large pockets to hold plenty of notions, plus a pincushion in the center to catch any stray pins that might otherwise get stuck in the arm of the chair!

Fabrics and Materials

Patterns, page 152
Pre-quilted fabric   ¼ yard
Light print   ¼ yard
Scraps of dk., med., lt., and white prints
6½" x 13" rectangle of muslin
6½" x 13" rectangle of batting
Polyester stuffing
1 package of ¼"-wide double-fold bias tape
Threads to match fabrics and bias tape

Pieces to Cut

6½" square	2 muslin
	2 batting
Template S2	6 lt. print
	5 med. print
	2 dk. print
	2 white print
Template T2	3 lt. print
	3 med. print
5½" x 7½" rectangle	1 lt. print
6½" x 20" rectangle	1 pre-quilted fabric

Instructions

1. Referring to Block Assembly diagram, join S2s and T2s as shown to make 1 Block 1 and 1 Block 2.
2. To make pockets: Layer 1 (6½") square of muslin, batting, and 1 pieced block (right side up) and pin. Repeat for second block. Machine-quilt in-the-ditch on each block. Using bias tape, bind 1 edge of each block. (This will be top edge of pocket.)
3. To make pincushion: With right sides facing and raw edges aligned, fold 5½" x 7½" rectangle in half lengthwise, forming a 2¾" x 7½" rectangle. Stitch long edges together. Turn and stuff firmly, leaving ¾" unstuffed at each end and centering seam.

4. Lay 6½" x 20" pre-quilted rectangle on table. With raw edges aligned, place pincushion (seam side down) across center of rectangle. Machine-baste each end of pincushion in place.
5. With raw edges aligned, pin 1 pocket right side up at each end of rectangle. Machine-baste around raw edges of each pocket.
6. Trim any uneven edges and bind outside edges of caddy with bias tape.

Block Assembly

Block 1

Block 2

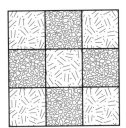

S2

T2

Light print

Med. print

White print

Dark print

Elegant Folded Bags

The Japanese art of folding paper to create beautiful gift cards and envelopes inspired these luxurious bags, which are simply folded from quilted squares. The lingerie bag is pieced from strips of white print fabric. It features an easy folded fabric rosebud and appliquéd leaves. (This project is great for using different white print strips left over from rotary cutting.) A richly colored border print fabric elegantly frames both the lingerie bag and the glasses case with mitered borders.

110

Rosebud Lingerie Bag

Fabrics and Materials

Muslin	½ yard
⅓ yard each of 3 assorted white prints	
Border print fabric	¼ yard
Gold print (for lining)	⅝ yard
Thick batting	18½" square
Scraps of red print, green print	
Scrap of freezer paper	
Thread to match fabrics and ribbon	
Green embroidery floss	
1½ yards (⅜"-wide) green grosgrain ribbon	

Pieces to Cut

4½" square	1 muslin
4½" x 22" strip	1 white print
2½" x 45" crosswise strip	2 different white prints
2½" x 20" strip	4 border print
18½" square	1 gold print

Instructions

1. Referring to Diagram A, Figure 1, lay 4½" x 22" white print strip, right side up, diagonally across 4½" muslin square, centering from corner to corner. Pin. With right sides facing and top raw edges aligned, lay 1 (2½"-wide) white print strip on top of first strip, trimming excess length. Stitch through all layers, as shown in Figure 2. Flip second strip right side up and press. Repeat, alternating 2½" white print strips until half of square is covered.

   Rotate square and repeat for other half, starting at 4½"-wide center strip and adding strips in same manner until entire square is covered. Turn square over and trim excess fabric even with muslin square. Press.

▶▶▶ TIME-SAVER

Instead of string piecing, you can simply use a 14½" white print square for the center of the bag. Continue the bag assembly by following the steps below.

2. Referring to Mitered Borders, page 147, join 4 border print strips to pieced square.
3. Stack batting, pieced block (right side up), and lining (right side down). Stitch along edges, leaving an opening for turning. Clip corners and turn. Slipstitch opening closed.
4. Referring to Machine Quilting, page 150, machine-quilt in-the-ditch around border. If desired, machine-quilt in-the-ditch along seams of string piecing.

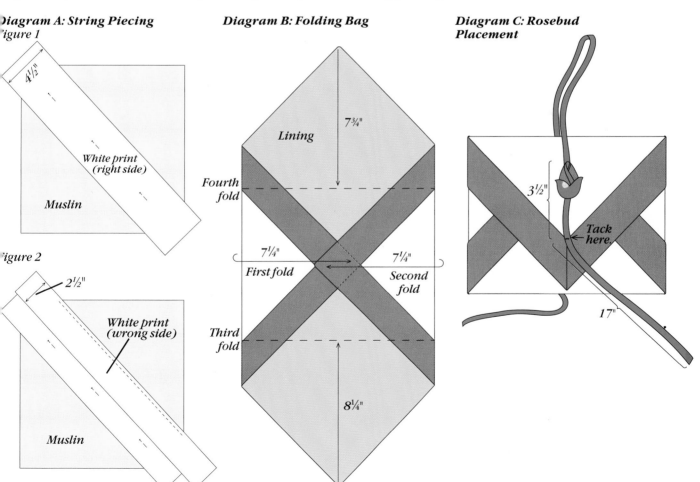

Diagram A: String Piecing
Figure 1

4½"

White print (right side)

Muslin

Figure 2

2½"

White print (wrong side)

Muslin

Diagram B: Folding Bag

Lining

7¾"

Fourth fold

7¼" First fold   7¼" Second fold

Third fold

8¼"

Diagram C: Rosebud Placement

3½"

Tack here.

17"

Glasses Case

Fabrics and Materials

White print	5" square
Gold print (for lining)	8" square
4 (2½" x 8") strips of border print	
Thick batting	8" square
Green embroidery floss	
Thread to match fabrics and ribbon	
18" (⅜"-wide) green grosgrain ribbon	
1 Velcro dot	

Instructions

1. Referring to Mitered Borders, page 147, join 4 border strips to white print square.
2. Stack batting, bordered square (right side up), and lining (right side down). Stitch along edges, leaving an opening for turning. Clip corners and turn. Slipstitch opening closed.
3. Machine-quilt in-the-ditch between border and square.
4. With lining side up, fold bag as shown in Diagram D. Using matching thread, slipstitch along edges of borders to join folded sides and bottom as shown.
  Referring to Embroidery Stitches, page 145, make 4 lazy daisy stitches on each side of glasses case as shown in Diagram.
5. Position hook side of Velcro dot 1" down from point of bottom fold and tack to secure. On lining, position loop side of Velcro dot 1" down from top point. Tack each to secure.
6. Tie ribbon in a bow. Referring to photo for placement and using matching thread, tack bow to glasses case through top layer only.

5. With lining side up, fold sides and bottom of bag as shown in Diagram B. Lightly press to set folds. Referring to Embroidery Stitches, page 145, make 4 lazy daisy stitches on each side of bag where borders meet. (See photo.) Referring to Diagram B, fold down top of bag. Lightly press.
6. To finish bag: Referring to Fabric Rosebuds, page 146, and using 3½" circle pattern on page 157, make 1 rosebud. Referring to Freezer Paper Appliqué, page 143, and using patterns on page 154, prepare 2 leaves and 1 calyx for appliqué.
  Measure 17" from 1 end of ribbon. Referring to Diagram C for placement and using thread to match ribbon, tack ribbon to bag, stitching through top layer only. Pull ribbon straight up over bag top as shown. Pin rosebud to bag and ribbon. Place calyx over bottom of rosebud. Using thread to match fabrics, appliqué calyx and then rosebud. Appliqué leaves. Wrap ribbon around back of bag and tie ends in a bow at bottom of appliquéd leaves. Trim ends of ribbon if necessary.

Diagram D:
Folding Glasses Case

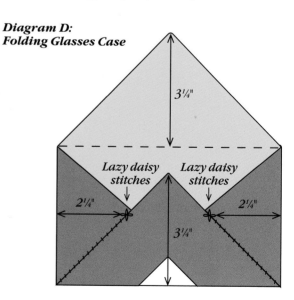

3¼"

Lazy daisy stitches   *Lazy daisy stitches*

2¼"   2¼"

3¼"

Antique Sewing Set

Suellen Wassem, of Beavercreek, Ohio, is a member of a group of designers known as Kindred Spirits. Their designs honor the heritage of traditional patchwork and recall pieces that were made long ago. In the old days, the fabric sewing box would have been made using the technique called "English piecing" (whipstitching scraps that were hand-basted around pattern pieces cut from paper). Suellen updated the method, but the charm of the patchwork box remains. A tiny Log Cabin block makes a useful pincushion and decorates the Heart-and-Hand Needle Keeper. Designed to resemble a treasured antique, the needle keeper combines symbols of love and friendship to make a gift that speaks without words.

Sewing Box

Fabrics and Materials

Scraps of 12 fabrics
Fusible fleece   ¼ yard
⅛"-wide satin ribbon   ½ yard
3 assorted buttons
Neutral thread

Pieces to Cut

Template A   24 fleece
6" length   3 ribbon

Instructions

1. Following manufacturer's instructions and spacing 1" apart, fuse 2 fleece pentagons to wrong sides of each of 12 different fabrics. Adding ½" seam allowances, cut out 24 pentagons.
2. Fold seam allowances under on all sides and press. Using a glue stick, adhere seam allowances to pentagons.
3. To make box lid: With wrong sides facing and edges aligned, place 1 pair of pentagons together. Referring to Diagram A, at 1 point of pentagon, insert 1 end of each of 3 ribbons ½" between layers. Leaving edge opposite this point open, slipstitch remaining 4 edges together, securing ends of ribbons in seam. On end of each ribbon, thread 1 button to about 2" from point of pentagon. Tie ribbon in a double knot at back of each button. Set aside.
4. With wrong sides facing, edges aligned, and matching pairs of fabric, use a glue stick to adhere remaining pairs of pentagons together.
5. Using neutral thread, make small, tight whipstitches through all layers to join 1 side of each of 5 pentagons to 1 center pentagon. (See Diagram B.)
    To form base of box: Align sides of adjacent pentagons and whipstitch together.
6. Referring to Figure 2, set in and whipstitch another pentagon between 2 pentagons on box base. Secure thread and clip.
    Referring to Figure 3, set in and whipstitch next pentagon along 3 edges as shown. Secure thread and clip.
    Join 3 remaining pentagons in same manner. Join edges of first and last pentagons together. When all pentagons have been joined, turn box right side out.
7. To join lid to box: Whipstitch open edge of lid to 1 edge of pentagon at top of box.

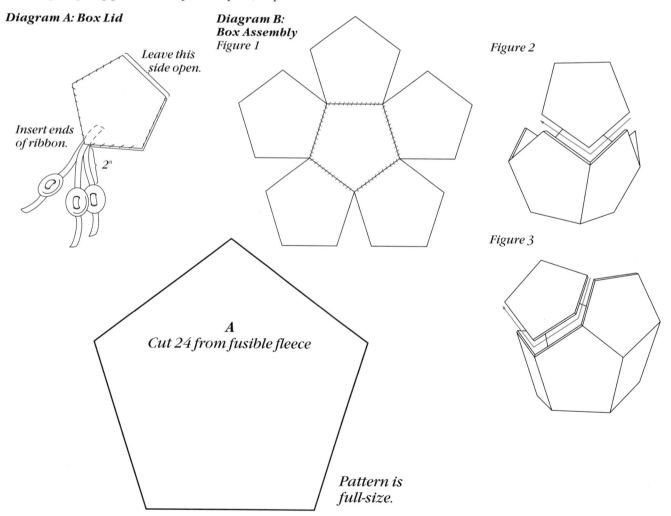

Diagram A: Box Lid

Leave this side open.

Insert ends of ribbon.

2"

Diagram B: Box Assembly
Figure 1

Figure 2

Figure 3

A
Cut 24 from fusible fleece

Pattern is full-size.

Log Cabin Pincushion

Fabrics and Materials

Scraps of dk. red, beige, tan, med. green, and dk. green prints
Polyester stuffing
Clean white sand (optional)
3 to 5 assorted buttons
Neutral thread

Pieces to Cut

1½" square	1 dk. red print
1½" x 4" strip	1 beige print
1½" x 6" strip	1 med. green print
1½" x 8" strip	1 tan print
1½" x 10" strip	1 dk. green print
5½" square	1 dk. red print

Instructions

1. Referring to Diagram A, Figure 1, with right sides facing and raw edges aligned, join beige strip to 1½" dark red center square. Trim strip to match length of center square. Fold strip out and press.

Referring to Figure 2, with right sides facing and raw edges aligned, join remainder of beige strip to top of red/beige unit and trim excess. Fold strip out and press.

2. Referring to red numerals in Diagram B for sequence, join strips counterclockwise to pieced unit, trimming to match length.

3. With right sides facing and raw edges aligned, join pieced block to 5½" dark red backing, leaving an opening for turning. Clip corners and turn. Stuff square firmly. *Hint: Add a handful of clean white sand along with the stuffing to give the pincushion more weight and stability.*

Slipstitch opening closed.

4. Referring to photo for placement, tack buttons to pincushion.

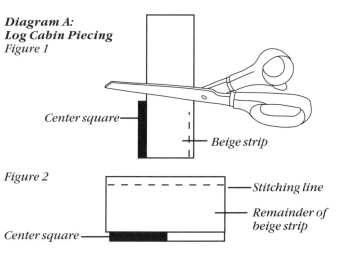

Diagram A:
Log Cabin Piecing
Figure 1

Center square —

— Beige strip

Figure 2

— Stitching line

— Remainder of beige strip

Center square —

Diagram B: Piecing Sequence

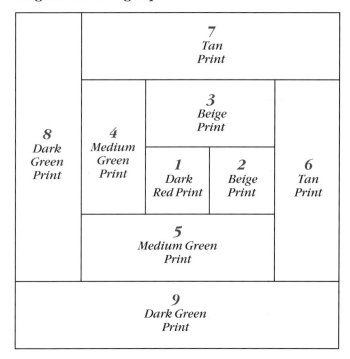

⭐ **BAZAAR TIP**

Good publicity is as important to the success of your bazaar as having wonderful items to sell. The more people who hear about the event, the greater the turnout will be. Spreading the word is the very important job of the publicity committee.

Newspapers and television stations can be a source of free publicity. Several weeks before the event, provide information for a suggested feature story. It could be about getting ready for the bazaar, a special craftsperson who will be exhibiting, or an unusual feature of your event. Type the information (using double spacing) and include all of the key facts, including the names of people to contact for further information. Include a photo or two if possible.

Many newspapers, radio, and television stations list upcoming events in free public service announcements. Contact *all* of them. There's no such thing as too much publicity!

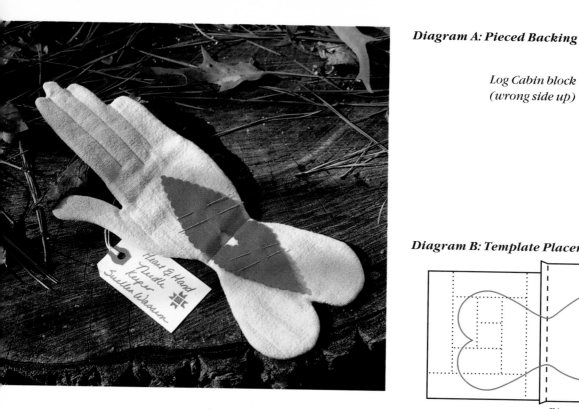

Log Cabin block
(wrong side up)

8"

6"

Diagram B: Template Placement

Pieced rectangle (wrong side up)

Heart-and-Hand Needle Keeper

Fabrics and Materials
Scraps of dk. red, beige, tan, med. green,
 and dk. green prints
Off-white osnaburg   ¼ yard
Scrap of red felt
Tracing paper
Yellow dressmaker's carbon
Neutral thread

Pieces to Cut
1½" square	1 dk. red print
1½" x 4" strip	1 beige print
1½" x 6" strip	1 med. green print
1½" x 8" strip	1 tan print
1½" x 10" strip	1 dk. green print
6" x 8" rectangle	1 osnaburg
6" x 13" rectangle	1 osnaburg
	1 batting
2¼" x 6½" rectangle	1 red felt

Instructions
1. Baste batting to wrong side of 6" x 13" osnaburg rectangle. Set aside.
2. Referring to Log Cabin Pincushion, Steps 1 through 3, make 1 (5½"-square) Log Cabin block.
3. Referring to Diagram A for placement, with right sides facing and raw edges aligned on 2 sides, stitch Log Cabin block to 6" x 8" osnaburg rectangle. Open up fabric and press seam toward Log Cabin block.
4. Using tracing paper, trace entire pattern, matching at large dots. Referring to Diagram B, position

pattern on wrong side of pieced rectangle, aligning large dots on seam and centering heart on Log Cabin block. Using dressmaker's carbon, transfer outline.
Hint: Template plastic, sold by the sheet at quilt shops and fabric stores, can be a great substitute for tissue paper patterns. Trace the pattern directly onto the plastic and cut it out on the traced line with a craft knife or scissors. Because the plastic is transparent, you'll be able to see where the seam line is on the pieced block for proper placement of the template.
5. With right sides facing and raw edges aligned, pin pieced rectangle to osnaburg/batting rectangle. Stitch on traced line, leaving an opening as shown on pattern for turning. Adding ¼" seam allowance, cut out. Clip curves almost to stitching line. Turn and press. Slipstitch opening closed.
6. On pieced side of hand, using a pencil and ruler, lightly draw topstitching lines to separate fingers. Topstitch along each line.
7. Fold felt in half widthwise to make a 2¼" x 3¼" rectangle. Transfer heart pattern to felt. Using pinking shears, cut out heart.

Place a pin through all layers to mark seam line joining Log Cabin block to hand. Turn over to unpieced side. Open out felt heart and align center fold of heart with pinned seam line. Pin heart in place. Turn back to pieced side, remove center pin, and stitch in-the-ditch along seam line. Remove remaining pins. Fold and gently press.

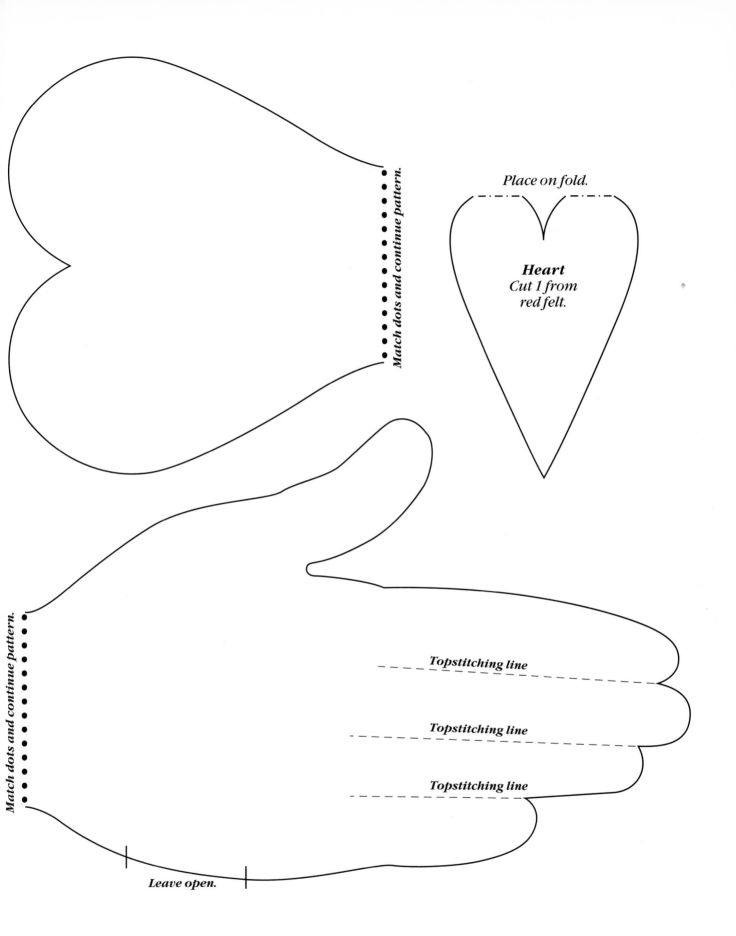

Match dots and continue pattern.

Place on fold.

Heart
Cut 1 from
red felt.

Match dots and continue pattern.

Topstitching line

Topstitching line

Topstitching line

Leave open.

Seminole Patchwork Shower Wraps

Cleo Le Vally, of Healdton, Oklahoma, is an expert on traditional Seminole piecing. She uses the patchwork designs in many ways and has discovered that these "his and her" shower wraps make wonderful wedding gifts. Quickly made using purchased towels, the rich colors and patterns of Seminole patchwork really makes them special.

Fabrics and Materials (for 1 wrap)
1 patchwork design (see instructions below)
30" x 54" bath towel*
Matching washcloth**
18" (¾"-wide) flat no-roll elastic
14" (¾"-wide) Velcro
Thread to match towel

*Note: For man's wrap, trim away 6" along 1 long edge (top) of towel. Set aside trimmed piece for man's optional pocket.

**Cut pocket for woman's wrap from matching washcloth, if desired.

Fabrics for patchwork design on man's wrap:
Blue	¼ yard
Cream	⅛ yard
Burgundy	⅛ yard
Neutral thread	

Fabrics for patchwork design on woman's wrap:
Rust	¼ yard
Gold	⅛ yard
Teal	⅛ yard
Neutral thread	

For Patchwork Design on Man's Wrap:
Pieces to Cut
2" x 45" crosswise strip	1 blue
	1 cream
1¾" x 45" crosswise strip	1 burgundy
¾" x 45" crosswise strip	2 burgundy
1¼" x 45" crosswise strip	2 blue

Instructions
1. Join 2" and 1¾" strips along long edges as shown in Diagram A, Figure 1. Cut across pieced band at 1¼" intervals.

Arrange these units, reversing position of colors and offsetting seams as shown in Figure 2. Join all units together in this manner.

2. Referring to Figure 3, trim points of patchwork band. For borders, with right sides facing and raw edges aligned, join 1 (¾"-wide) burgundy strip to patchwork band along each long edge. With right sides facing and raw edges aligned, join 1 (1¼"-wide) blue strip to burgundy along each long edge.

3. On each long edge, turn raw edge under ¼". Press.

Diagram A: Patchwork Design for Man's Wrap
Figure 1

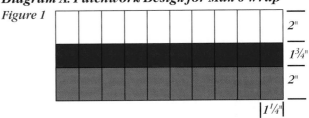

Figure 2

Reverse units and offset centers, matching seams.

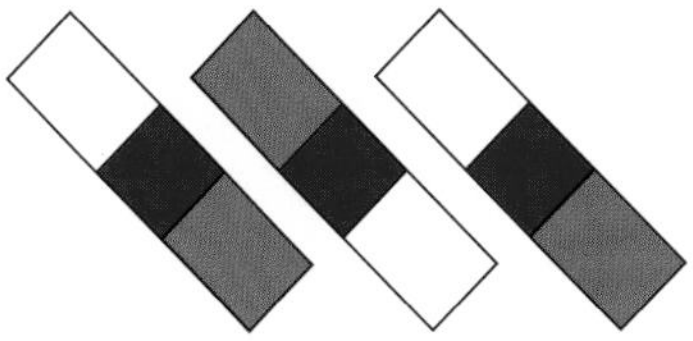

Figure 3

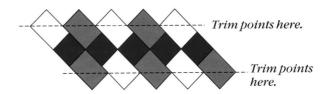

Trim points here.

Trim points here.

For Patchwork Design on Woman's Wrap:
Pieces to Cut
3" x 45" crosswise strip	2 rust
¾" x 45" crosswise strip	1 teal
	2 gold
1¼" x 45" crosswise strip	1 gold
	2 teal

Instructions
1. Join 2 (3-wide") rust, 1 (¾"-wide) teal, and 1 (1¼"-wide) gold strips along long edges as shown in Diagram B, Figure 1.

2. With 45° line on quilter's ruler aligned with bottom edge of pieced band, cut across band at 45° angle at 2" intervals as shown in Figure 2.

3. Rearrange units side by side, with pattern offset up as shown in Figure 3. Match seams and join.

4. Referring to Figure 4, trim points of patchwork band. With right sides facing and raw edges aligned, join 1 (¾"-wide) gold strip to patchwork

Diagram B: Patchwork Design for Woman's Wrap

Figure 1

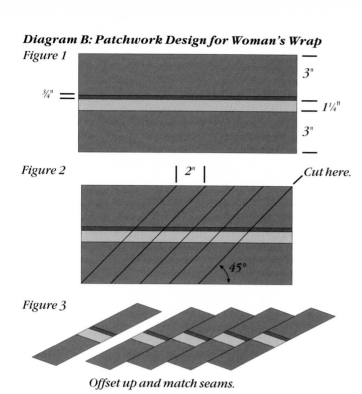

¾" =   3"
              1¼"
              3"

Figure 2

| 2" | Cut here.

45°

Figure 3

Offset up and match seams.

Figure 4

Trim points here.

Trim points here.

band along each long edge. For borders, with right sides facing and raw edges aligned, join 1 (1¼"-wide) teal strip to gold along each long edge.
5. On each long edge, turn raw edge under ¼". Press.

To assemble shower wrap:
Instructions
1. With wrong sides facing, fold towel into quarters widthwise. Mark quarters with pins. Unfold. Align 1 end of Seminole patchwork design with top long edge of towel, 3" from right edge of towel; pin design to towel. Trim bottom of patchwork design 2" longer than towel. Turn bottom raw edge of patchwork design under ¼". Press. Fold excess patchwork design to wrong side of wrap and pin to towel. On right side of towel, topstitch long edges of patchwork design to towel. Turn towel over and slipstitch end of patchwork design to wrong side of towel.
2. To attach elastic: On wrong side of wrap, center elastic horizontally ¼" from top edge of towel, extending slightly beyond first pin and third pin. (See Diagram C.) Topstitch 1 end of elastic to towel. Topstitch again to reinforce. Repeat to topstitch opposite end. Remove pins.
   For casing, turn under ¼" and then 1¼" along top edge of towel and press. Topstitch across towel, 1⅛" from top.

3. Referring to Diagram D for placement, stitch loop side of Velcro to wrong side of casing. On right side, at other end of wrap, stitch hook side of Velcro.
4. To add optional pocket: For man's wrap, cut a 6" x 8½" rectangle from trimmed piece of towel. Zigzag raw edges. On 2 long edges and 1 end, turn under ¼". Press. On remaining end, turn under ¼" and then 1¼". Topstitch across pocket, 1⅛" from top edge of pocket.
   Position pocket on right side of wrap, 7" from top edge and 13½" from right edge of wrap. Topstitch 3 sides of pocket to wrap.
   For woman's wrap, use matching washcloth to make pocket as above. Position pocket 13½" from top edge and 13½" from right edge of wrap. Topstitch as above.

Diagram C: Wrap Assembly

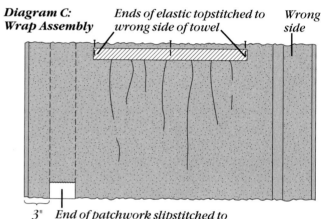

Ends of elastic topstitched to wrong side of towel   Wrong side

3"   End of patchwork slipstitched to wrong side of towel

Diagram D Velcro Placement

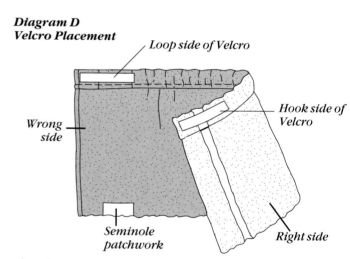

Loop side of Velcro

Hook side of Velcro

Wrong side

Seminole patchwork   Right side

⭐ **BAZAAR TIP**
These Seminole patchwork designs can also turn plain place mats into exciting bazaar best-sellers. Or, pieced in soft pastels, the designs can be used to decorate purchased pillow cases or guest towels. Each band will make a patchwork design about 1 yard long.

Vintage Accessories

Alice Strebel and Sally Korte, of Kindred Spirits in Dayton, Ohio, design clothing and accessories with an antique look. Fabric roses, quickly gathered from scrap strips, are tacked to a purchased doily to make a corsage that can be fastened at the neck of a blouse, on a belt, or pinned to a hat. The patchwork belt is reminiscent of old-fashioned Postage Stamp quilts that were made from hundreds of tiny scrap squares. Both of these projects make good use of strips left from rotary cutting. And the embroidered heart pin turns a small scrap of fabric into a keepsake.

Rose Corsage

Fabrics and Materials
Pattern, page 124
Tracing paper
1 (3¼" x 14") strip each of 3 assorted prints
Scraps of dk. green print
6" round crocheted doily
Thread to match fabrics
1"-long pin fastener
Hot-glue gun and glue sticks (optional)

Instructions
1. Using tracing paper and matching dots, trace rose pattern. With right sides facing and raw edges aligned, fold 1 (3¼" x 14") strip in half widthwise to measure 3¼" x 7". Trace pattern on wrong side of folded fabric and cut out. Unfold.
2. With right sides facing and raw edges aligned, fold strip in half lengthwise. Referring to Diagram, stitch as shown, leaving an opening for turning. Clip as shown on pattern and turn. Turn under raw edges ¼". Do not press. Run a gathering thread ⅛" from straight edge, catching turned-under edges in stitching. Pull gathers so that strip measures 5". Fasten off. Starting at 1 end, roll gathered strip into a rose-shaped coil. Use hot-glue gun or tack through all layers to secure. Repeat to make 2 more fabric roses. Set roses aside.

Diagram: Stitching Rose Strip

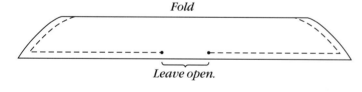

Fold

Leave open.

3. Trace leaf pattern 6 times on wrong side of dark green scrap and cut out. With right sides facing and raw edges aligned, pin 2 leaf pieces together. Stitch, leaving straight edge open for turning. Trim seam to ⅛". Turn and press. Repeat to make 2 more leaves.
4. Arrange roses and leaves on doily. Remove roses and set aside. Using hot-glue gun or stitching by hand, first secure each leaf and then each rose to doily.
5. Center pin fastener on back of doily, 1½" from top of doily. Use hot-glue gun or tack to secure pin fastener.

Keepsake Heart Pin

Fabrics and Materials
Pattern, page 124
Scrap of osnaburg
Embroidery floss: dk. green, red
Thread to match fabric
3 assorted buttons
Polyester stuffing
1"-long pin fastener
Hot-glue gun and glue sticks (optional)

Instructions
1. Trace heart pattern 2 times on osnaburg. On 1 heart, lightly trace stem design. Referring to Embroidery Stitches, page 145, and using 6 strands of dark green floss, embroider stems and leaves with backstitch. Using red floss, sew 1 button at top of each stem for flowers. Cut out both hearts.
2. With right sides facing and raw edges aligned, stitch hearts together, leaving an opening for turning. Referring to pattern, clip almost to seam at top of heart. Turn and stuff firmly. Slipstitch opening closed.
3. Center pin fastener on back of heart, 1¼" from top of lobes. Use hot-glue gun or tack to secure pin fastener.

Patchwork Belt

Fabrics and Materials
Patterns, pages 124 and 125
1 (1½" x 12") strip each of 8 med. and dk. assorted prints
Scrap of lt. brown osnaburg
Brown print   ¼ yard
Embroidery floss: dk. green, tan
2 (3½") lengths of ⅝"-wide cotton lace
7" (¾"-wide) Velcro
2¼" (⅛"-wide) elastic
3 assorted buttons

Pieces to Cut
2¼" x 11½" strip	4 brown print (backs, linings)
Template A	1 brown print (front lining)
Template B	2 patchwork (side front panel)
Template C	1 osnaburg (center front panel)

Instructions
1. To make patchwork: Join 1½" x 12" strips along long edges as shown in Diagram A, Figure 1. Cut across pieced band at 1½" intervals as shown.
Referring to Figure 2, arrange these units, reversing position of colors. Stitch strips together along long edges. Trace Template B 2 times on patchwork as shown and cut out. Set aside.

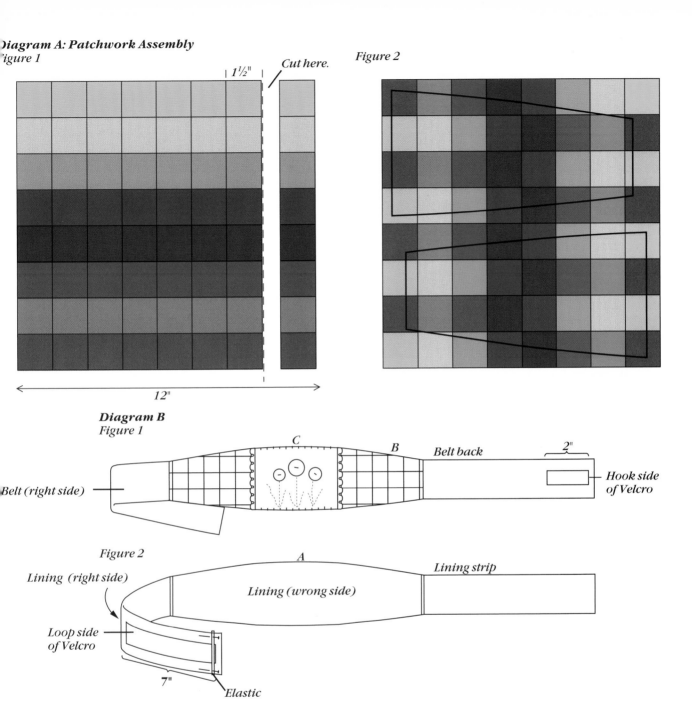

Diagram A: Patchwork Assembly
Figure 1

1½"

Cut here.

Figure 2

12"

Diagram B
Figure 1

Belt (right side)

C

B

Belt back

2"

Hook side of Velcro

Figure 2

A

Lining (right side)

Lining strip

Lining (wrong side)

Loop side of Velcro

Elastic

7"

2. To make embroidered center front panel: With right sides facing and raw edges aligned, baste 1 length of lace to each end of osnaburg (C). On right side of C, lightly trace design for embroidery. Referring to Embroidery Stitches, page 145, and using 6 strands of dark green floss, embroider stems and leaves with backstitch and then sew 1 button at top of each stem for flowers.

3. To assemble belt: With right sides facing and raw edges aligned, join 1 B to C, catching lace in seam. Repeat on opposite side. With right sides facing and raw edges aligned, join 1 (2¼" x 11½") belt back to each end of patchwork belt front. Referring to Diagram B, Figure 1, with right side up, stitch 2"-long piece of hook side of Velcro to belt back, ¾" from end.

With right sides facing and raw edges aligned, join 1 (2¼" x 11½") lining strip to each end of lining (A). Referring to Figure 2, with right side of lining up, stitch a 7"-long piece of loop side of Velcro to belt lining. For belt loop, with raw edges aligned, place elastic at end of Velcro, across strip. Pin.

With right sides facing, raw edges aligned, and Velcro at opposite ends, place belt on lining and stitch, catching ends of elastic in seams and leaving an opening for turning. Clip corners, turn, and press. Slipstitch opening closed.

4. Referring to Embroidery Stitches, page 145, use 6 strands of tan floss to embroider blanket stitch along top and bottom edge of center front panel.

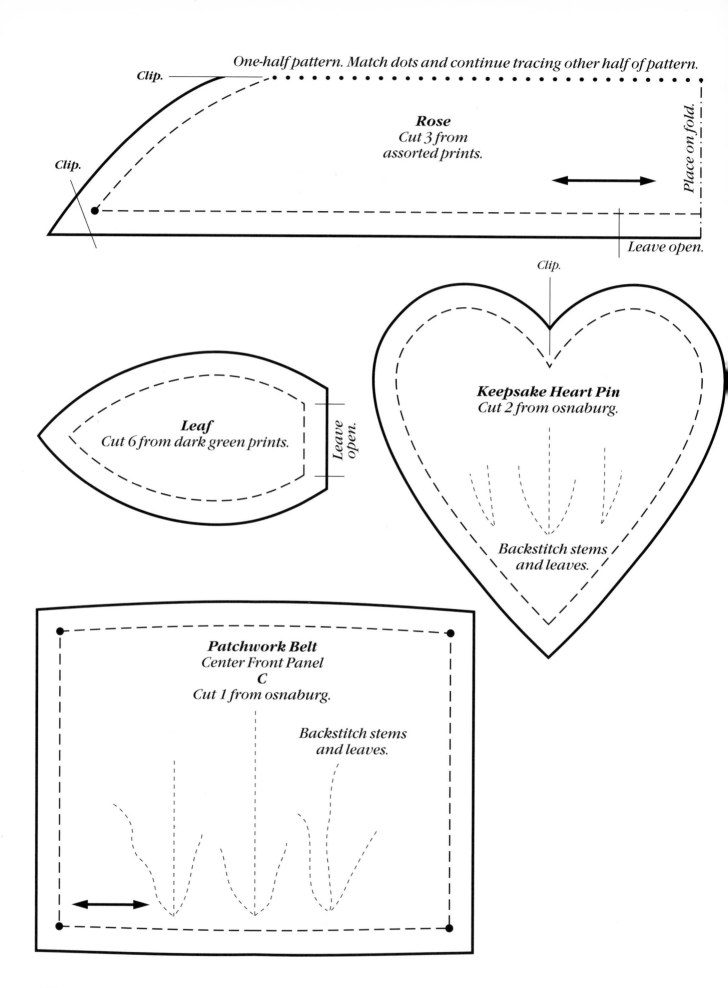

One-half pattern. Match dots and continue tracing other half of pattern.

Clip.

Clip.

Rose
*Cut 3 from
assorted prints.*

Place on fold.

Leave open.

Clip.

Leaf
Cut 6 from dark green prints.

Leave open.

Keepsake Heart Pin
Cut 2 from osnaburg.

*Backstitch stems
and leaves.*

Patchwork Belt
*Center Front Panel
C
Cut 1 from osnaburg.*

*Backstitch stems
and leaves.*

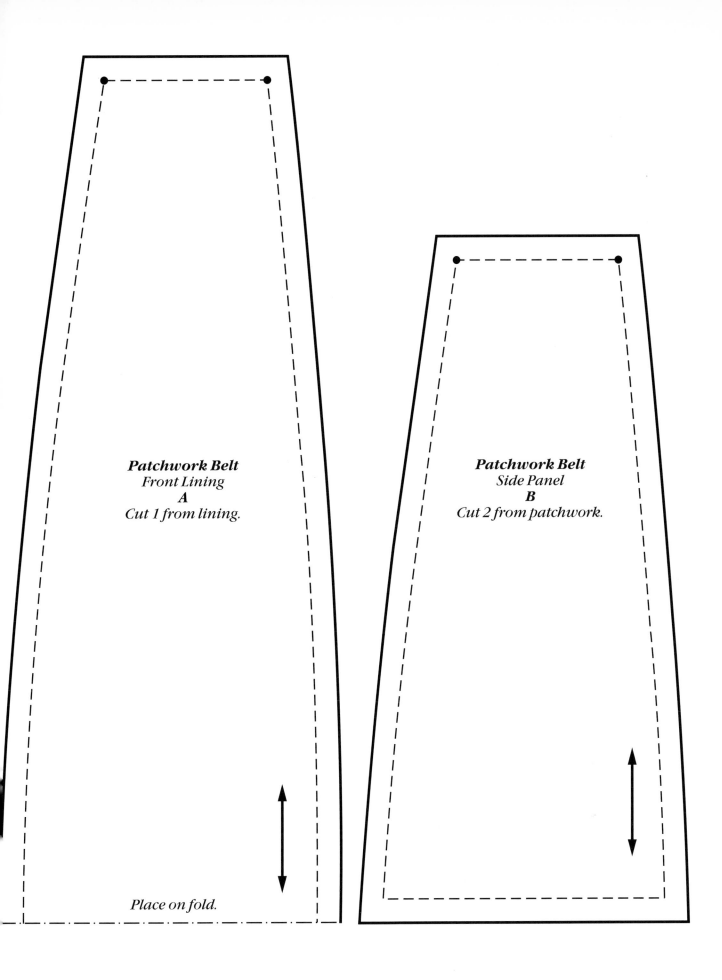

Patchwork Belt
Front Lining
A
Cut 1 from lining.

Place on fold.

Patchwork Belt
Side Panel
B
Cut 2 from patchwork.

Kitchen Towel
Eileen Westfall

Bazaar Fun Raisers

Fun raisers are special touches that add fun to your bazaar (and funds, as well). We'll show you how to create the cover for your own bazaar cookbook, shopping bags, colorful tags, and a bright bazaar banner. Your group can turn small scraps into a sensational fund-raising quilt. You'll find suggestions for "little extras" that will make your event a favorite with bazaargoers, and there are ideas for other activities that will add to your profits and promote your bazaar.

Bazaar Planning

Abazaar can be held by small groups of volunteers who create items to sell and then donate all of the profits. Or it can be a large craft fair, exhibiting the work of skilled artisans who rent booths and contribute a portion of their sales to the sponsoring organization.

Whether the event is large or small, all successful bazaars require planning and organization. Though all bazaars are different, here are some guidelines to get you started toward your very best bazaar!

Start planning early. If your bazaar is an annual event, begin planning the next one immediately afterward by evaluating your sales and other aspects. If this is your first bazaar, plan the date carefully in conjunction with other community events. The holiday season seems ideal for holding a bazaar, but if there are already many other activities scheduled in your town, your group might decide to have a springtime or autumn bazaar.

Elect a general chairperson and the heads of all committees. There should be committees for each of the booths, publicity, decorations, and set-up. You may want other committees as well to plan activities for children, a raffle, a bake sale, or other refreshments to sell. All of the committees should start organizing and gathering volunteers early.

Pick a winning theme. It isn't necessary for a successful bazaar to have a theme, but it's so much more fun! Your theme can be the key to decorations and publicity, and it can be a way to coordinate a great array of projects. You might choose a motif such as baskets, birds, or bears. Or your theme could be a phrase such as "The Holly and the Ivy," "Hearts and Flowers," or "Holidays Around the World." A successful theme will bring pleasant images to mind, but still leave room for surprises.

Elect a pricing committee. It's the best way to set a fair price for your wares. The committee can consider the cost of materials, the quality of the work, and the time involved in making the item. They can then set the best price, knowing of course, that most bazaargoers are searching for bargains!

Plan simple, attractive displays that will be easy to set up and take down. They should be as simple and inexpensive as possible. Cover folding tables with sheets. Use rungs of stepladders as shelves for displays. Branches of evergreens in vases make the perfect background for hanging Christmas ornaments.

Take care of the practical details well in advance of the event. Determine how much space you will have and decide how many booths the space can comfortably accommodate. Arrange to rent additional folding tables or other items. Check on local safety code requirements with your fire department. Make arrangements for parking and, if necessary, contact your police department for help with controlling traffic.

Great Graphics

Patchwork designs are a natural starting point for easy, great-looking graphics for your bazaar. For a coordinated, well-planned look, choose a color scheme using no more than three colors. Select a patchwork motif to serve as a distinctive bazaar logo and use it throughout the bazaar on banners, signs, price tags, and decorations.

This weather-resistant banner has an easy sponge-painted patchwork border. Sponge painting can also be used to decorate shopping bags, which can be sold at a nominal price. And stencils make it simple to produce lots of attractive price tags in just minutes.

You can raise extra money for your bazaar by collecting tried-and-true favorite recipes and selling your own bazaar cookbook. Use fabric scraps to make an attractive design for a cover that can be reproduced very inexpensively. Working with your local printer or copy shop, you can save on expenses by doing much of the graphic preparation on your own.

Bazaar Banner

Fabrics and Materials

Heavy canvas	1½ yards

Thread to match canvas
Acrylic paints: red, gold, blue (or your bazaar's colors)
A shallow dish
2 sponges (at least 4" wide)
Purchased stencils for lettering*
Masking tape
6 (¾"-diameter) plastic curtain rings

Note: Stencils for letters spelling "Bazaar" in photo are 10" high. (You may prefer to stencil the entire name of your bazaar by using smaller stencils and placing them on two lines.) Space available for lettering inside borders is 39½" x 16½".

Instructions
1. Cut canvas to measure 26½" x 54". Turn under ¼" on all sides. Press. Using matching thread, topstitch. Referring to Diagram A, Figure 1, lightly draw lines 3" from top and bottom edges and 4½" from each side.

Diagram A: Placement Lines
Figure 1

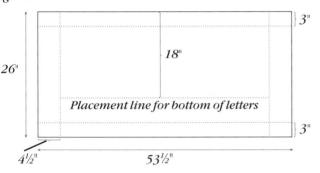

2. For 10"-high letters, lightly draw a horizontal line 18" from top of banner as shown, for positioning stenciled letters. (If you have chosen a different-size stencil, draw horizontal base line for positioning letters as desired.) Aligning bottom of letters with drawn line, position stencils, centering word widthwise. Tape stencils securely to canvas.
3. Referring to Stenciling, page 143, pour red acrylic paint into a shallow dish and stencil each letter, using stencil brush or sponge. Allow to dry completely before removing stencils.
4. For borders, cut 1 (3½") square and 2 (2") squares from sponges. Cut 1 (2") sponge in half diagonally to make 2 triangles. For corner star, referring to Sponge-painting, page 143, and to Figure 2 for placement, use 3½" sponge and blue paint to sponge-paint 1 square in each corner as shown. Let dry. Using triangle sponge and gold paint, sponge-paint 8 triangles around each square as shown. Let dry.

Figure 2

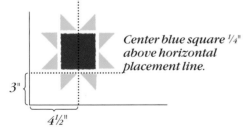

Center blue square ¼" above horizontal placement line.

Referring to photo for placement and using 2"-square sponges, add blue checkerboard design, using drawn lines as guides.
5. Tack plastic rings to top back edge of banner.

Decorated Shopping Bags

Fabrics and Materials (for 1 bag)
(Bags shown in photo at beginning of this chapter.)
1 shopping bag or small gift bag
  (may be plain or coated paper)
Acrylic paints in colors of choice
Shallow dish
2 (2"-square) sponges

Instructions
1. Cut 1 sponge in half diagonally to make 2 triangles.
2. Use sponges as described in Bazaar Banner, Step 4 to decorate shopping bags or small gift bags. Diagram B shows several designs that can be made using squares and triangles. Experiment with additional combinations as desired.

Diagram B: Sponge Paint Designs

Bazaar Price Tags

Fabrics and Materials
(Tags are shown in the photo at the beginning of this chapter.)
Plain 2⅜" x 4¾" tie-on tags (available at office supply stores)
Plastic template material or used manila file folders
Craft knife
Fine-point felt tip markers

Instructions
1. Trace several stencil designs on template material or recycled file folders, spacing designs at least 2" apart. Cut designs apart. Using craft knife, cut out on design lines to make stencils.
2. Working on a flat surface, center stencil about ¼" from straight end of tag. Holding stencil firmly with left hand and using fine-point marker, trace outlines of stencil design. Remove stencil and fill in design.
3. Complete tag by writing name of project, name of crafter (if desired), and price. Tie tag to project or attach with small safety pin.
Hint: We use tie-on tags for most patchwork projects because the adhesive from stick-on tags may leave a residue on some fabrics.

Patchwork Stencil Designs
Stencil patterns are full-size.

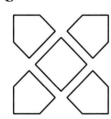
A

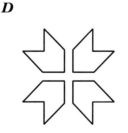
B

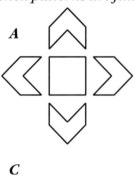
C

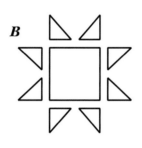
D

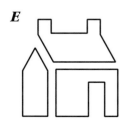
E

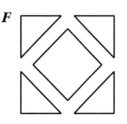
F

BAZAAR TIP
You can use these stencil designs as graphic elements for printed material such as raffle tickets, postcards, and fliers. Using a fine-point black marker, trace the stencil outline on white paper and then fill in the design. Use this black-and-white art when pasting up material to be printed.

Best Bazaar Cookbook

Fabrics and Materials (for 5½" x 8½" cookbook cover)
Pattern, page 157
Scraps of 2 bright plaid or checked fabrics
Paper-backed fusible web
8½" x 11" sturdy white paper
Non-photo blue pencil (available at art supply stores)
Felt-tip calligraphy pen
or
Press-down type (available at art supply stores)
Note: Size of type will be determined by length of cookbook title. Sketch a full-size cover with all graphic elements in place in order to choose correct type size. Take this mock-up with you when you go to buy the type.

Instructions
1. Trace house pattern on paper side of fusible web. Following manufacturer's instructions, fuse web to wrong side of first fabric scrap and cut out. On paper side of remaining fusible web, draw 2 (1") squares. Fuse squares to wrong side of second fabric scrap. Cut out. Cut each square in half diagonally to make 2 triangles. Remove paper backings from all pieces. Set aside.
2. Referring to Diagram C, use non-photo blue pencil to draw placement lines on 8½" x 11" paper as indicated.

Diagram C: Cover Placement Lines

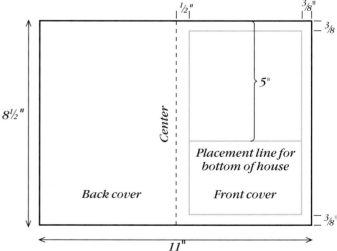

Fun Raising Activities

Along with wonderful handmade items, the most successful bazaars often have special activities that help keep customers coming back year after year. Bazaar planners all around the country shared with us their favorite successful ideas for increasing the fun and raising funds as well.

3. Referring to photo and aligning raw edges with marked corners, position 1 triangle in 1 corner. Using *dry* iron, fuse triangle to paper. Repeat to use remaining corner triangles.

Aligning bottom of house with placement line, position house and fuse to paper.

4. Using calligraphy pen, letter cookbook title in space below house. Or, following manufacturer's instructions, place press-down type in that space.

5. At the copy shop, choose the color and type of paper for the cookbook cover. You may select card stock or use standard weight paper. Your copies will be in black ink unless the copy shop has another choice of ink.

6. For recipe pages in cookbook, check with your printer or copy shop for advice. Type recipes to fit vertically on each half of 8½" x 11" paper. Plan to photocopy recipes on both sides of paper to make pages for cookbook. Insert pages inside cover, staple down center through all layers, and fold to make a book.

Offer small free cups of hot cider, tea, or coffee to welcome bazaargoers. Many bazaars make extra money by selling small bags of cider spices and cards with recipes for spiced cider or tea.

Award door prizes several times every day. Everyone loves the chance to be a winner.

Have volunteers demonstrate quilting, stenciling, or other crafts that were used to make your wares. Bazaargoers enjoy talking with crafters and learning more about how the projects are made. Besides the completed craft items, kits with pre-cut pieces for patchwork pillows, pincushions, or doll quilts (page 52–54) can be sold as well.

Provide a gentle musical background. A harp, a piano, or a quartet of singers making *very soft* music can add a festive atmosphere.

If your bazaar charges an admission fee, reduce or eliminate the fee for those who bring a donation of non-perishable food. Collect the food for a food bank or shelter.

Have a silent auction. Display several great projects along with sheets where bids can be written down. (To be sure that items are purchased at a fair price, minimum bids may be set.) As the amount of the bids increases, bazaargoers can return to make new bids until the auction ends.

A "free-for-all" auction can be a fun way to sell chances on several small items. (It's really a raffle, so check the laws in your state to be sure you don't violate any of them!) Display five small items. Place a basket in front of each one. Then sell tickets in sets of five. The bazaargoer may put one ticket in each basket or increase the chances of winning a particular item by placing several tickets in one basket.

A preview party, with refreshments donated by sponsors or volunteers, can raise a lot of extra money and become an annual event that people look forward to. Many people will gladly pay an extra admission fee for a "private showing," perhaps the evening before the bazaar officially begins.

For a small preview party, a limited number of tickets may be sold in advance, or you may send invitations to people on a special mailing list. For larger crowds, advertise the preview party, including the special admission price.

Scrappy Fabric Bows

For the most successful bazaar, you want every scrap to count. These pretty stiffened bows can be made from left-over strips of fabric in assorted lengths and widths. Sell them as decorative accents or add them to other items for sale at your bazaar. Christmas reds and greens are natural for holiday wreaths. Soft pastel colors and country prints make attractive additions to baskets and dried flower arrangements.

Fabric and Materials (for 1 bow)
Strip of fabric
Fabric stiffener
1" paintbrush
10" florist's wire
Newspaper
Waxed paper
Aluminum foil
Wooden clip-type clothespins

Instructions
1. Trim fabric strip if necessary so that edges are parallel and straight. Press strip.
2. Cover work table with newspaper. Place a long strip of waxed paper on newspaper. Lay fabric (right side down) on waxed paper.
3. Stir fabric stiffener and pour some into a small bowl. Using paintbrush, paint fabric generously with stiffener.
4. With wrong sides facing, fold strip lengthwise, bringing long raw edges together in center. Using clothespin at 1 end, hang strip outside on clothesline until damp-dry (about ½ hour).
5. For bow center, cut 2" piece from 1 end of strip and set aside.
6. Referring to Diagram, Figure 1, arrange strip as shown. Wrap florist's wire around center of strip as shown in Figure 2. Twist wire together at center of bow, leaving an equal length of wire free at each end. Bend wire to center back of bow and twist wire together. With paintbrush, apply additional stiffener to bow center. Wrap the 2" piece of fabric around bow center, covering twist of wire. Overlap ends at back and apply more stiffener on overlapped area.

Figure 2

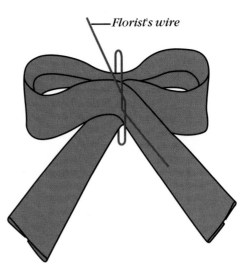
Florist's wire

7. Lay bow on waxed paper. Twist and shape loops and tails as desired. Trim ends of tails as shown in photo. Wad aluminum foil into balls and insert under curves of tails and in loops of bow to hold them open while stiffener dries. Allow bow to dry. If desired, apply a second coat of stiffener to bow.

BAZAAR TIP
As you make items for your bazaar, be sure to save all those scraps! In addition to the fabric bows above, you'll find many projects in this book that use small scraps.

You can also use those scraps to decorate brightly colored aprons for the workers at your bazaar. Use paper-backed fusible web to adhere assorted print scraps in patchwork designs to solid-colored purchased aprons. The green apron pictured at the beginning of this chapter features a simple design made from triangles and one square. Choose a similar patchwork design or use your bazaar logo.

And of course, save all of your small scraps to make a group fund-raising quilt like the one shown on the next page.

Diagram: Making a Bow
Figure 1

Wrong side

Right side

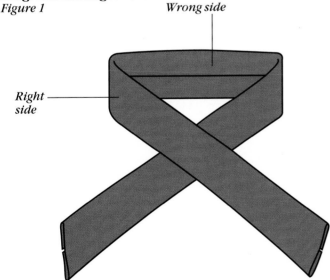

Grand Prize Quilt

Joan McGlaughlin, from Fishing Creek, Maryland, made this stunning wall quilt featuring 648 *different* fabrics and only one template. Because all of those different prints really make the overall pattern sparkle, and because of the way the blocks are assembled, this is an excellent quilt for a group to make.

Working together on a fund-raising quilt can be one of the most successful and satisfying activities. Group members can choose prints from their own scrap bags to make units and then combine the units to make the quilt. The members can have an old-fashioned quilting bee to baste the completed quilt top and to add the quilting.

Finished Size
Quilt: 52" x 52"
Blocks: 9 (15" x 15")

Fabrics and Materials
Pattern, page 138

Scraps of assorted dk. prints	2 yards
Scraps of assorted med. prints	½ yard
Scraps of assorted lt. prints	1 yard
Dk. green	1¾ yards
Backing	3½ yards
Batting	1 twin-size
Neutral thread, dk. green thread	

Pieces to Cut

Template A*	324 dk. assorted
	108 med. assorted
	216 lt. assorted
4" x 60" strip (for borders)	4 dk. green
2" x 56" strip (for binding)	4 dk. green

▶▶▶ TIME-SAVER
*You can cut accurate triangles quickly from squares, without using the pattern. Cut a 3⅜" square. Then cut the square in half diagonally to yield two triangles.

Instructions
1. Referring to Diagram A for placement and using neutral thread, join 9 dark, 3 medium, and 6 light triangles together to make 1 unit. Repeat to make 35 more units.
2. Referring to Diagram B, join 4 units to make 1 block, placing units so that dark triangles meet in center as shown. Repeat to make 8 more 4-unit blocks.

Diagram A: Unit Assembly

Join 9 dark, 3 medium, and 6 light triangles to make 1 unit. Make 36 units.

7½" (8" with seam allowance)

Diagram B: Block Assembly

15" (15½" with seam allowance)
Join 4 units to make 1 block. Make 9 blocks.

3. Referring to photo, join 3 blocks to make 1 vertical row. Repeat to make 2 more 3-block rows. Join rows together.
4. Referring to Mitered Borders, page 147, and using thread to match, join 4" x 60" dark green borders to sides, top, and bottom of quilt, mitering corners.

6. Trace Heart Quilting Pattern in center of each 4-unit block. Quilt hearts and quilt in-the-ditch around all remaining triangles. Quilt borders as desired. Trim backing and batting even with quilt top when quilting is completed. Set aside trimmed backing to make hanging sleeve.

Referring to Binding, page 150, piece 4 (2" x 56") dark green strips to make straight-grain binding. Bind quilt. Using reserved backing fabric, add hanging sleeve to back.

BAZAAR TIP

Selling chances on a quilt usually raises more money than simply selling the quilt outright. At nearly every quilt show these days, you'll find either a raffle or a donation quilt. If you plan to raffle a quilt, be sure you know about the laws regarding raffles in your state.

Once you understand the legal requirements, it is best to start selling tickets for the raffle a few weeks before your bazaar begins. Distribute tickets along with some photos of the quilt to your bazaar volunteers for early ticket sales. You may be able to arrange to display the quilt in a local store window. Not only will you sell more raffle tickets, you'll also create interest and publicity for your bazaar.

5. For pieced backing, cut 3½ yards of backing fabric in half widthwise to measure 1¾ yards. With right sides facing and raw edges aligned, join along long edge. Cut backing and batting to size of quilt top plus 4" all around. Place backing (right side down) on a flat surface. Center and stack batting and pieced quilt top (right side up) on backing. Referring to Basting with Safety Pins, page 148, pin-baste layers together.

Heart Quilting Pattern

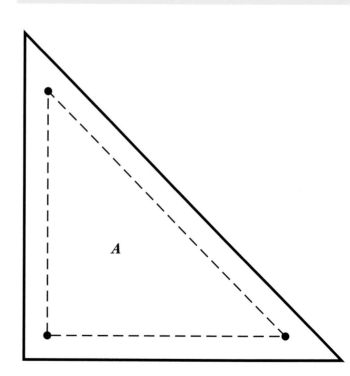

A

Patchwork Basics

I f you are new to patchwork, here are some things you'll need to know before you get started. Information on specific techniques follows, as well as all the patterns that were used in the *Star Harvest Sampler* quilt blocks and other projects.

Getting Started

Fabrics

The best fabric for patchwork and quilting is 100% cotton. Since our bazaar projects are designed to save time, it is best to avoid directional or one-way prints. Fabric requirements are based on 44"–45"-wide fabric and allow for shrinkage. The selvage should not be used in piecing.

The lengthwise and crosswise fabric threads form the grain of the fabric. Lengthwise grain (parallel to the selvages) has the least stretch; crosswise grain has a little more give. Long borders should be cut on the lengthwise grain. Other pieces with straight sides can be cut with one side aligned with either the lengthwise or crosswise grain. The diagonal grain of the fabric is called the "bias." It has the greatest amount of stretch and is used for pieces that curve.

The fabric should be machine-washed, dried, and pressed before cutting. Use warm water and detergent but do not use fabric softener. For certain projects (such as those that will never be washed and will not be hand-quilted), you may skip this step.

Batting

Polyester batting is the best choice for the projects in this book. Lightweight low-loft batting works well for hand quilting, while thick batting is perfect for tied quilts or comforters. For small projects, buy a crib-size sheet of batting. Use loose polyester filler for stuffing such projects as the Patchwork Cat and Calico Angel Ornaments.

Seam allowance

Seam allowances are ¼", unless otherwise noted. All full-size patterns for piecing, patterns placed on grids, and measurements for pieces, sashing, and borders include ¼" seam allowances, unless otherwise noted. *Patterns for appliqué do not include seam allowances.*

Enlarging patterns

Most patterns in this book are full-size, but a few had to be reduced to fit on these pages. The quickest way to enlarge the patterns is to take the book to a photocopy shop. Though all the patterns are protected under copyright by Oxmoor House, permission for photocopying is given on these particular patterns so that you may enlarge them for your personal use. The pattern instructions will tell the percentage of enlargement to request.

If a photocopier is not available, you can easily enlarge the pattern yourself. First, you will need to draw a grid. (Using graph paper or gridded freezer paper will save time and ensure that the squares are accurate.) Directions on the gridded pattern will tell you how large the squares in your grid should be. Copy 1 square at a time from the small grid in the book to the larger grid you have made. Each large square on your grid should contain the same shape as that shown in each small square in the book.

Making templates and marking fabric

A template is a pattern shape made from a sturdy material. Trace the pattern directly onto plastic template material, or make a template by tracing the pattern onto paper and gluing the paper to posterboard or sandpaper. (Sandpaper will not slip when placed on fabric.) Cut the template on the marked line, using a craft knife or sharp paper-cutting scissors. It is very important that the template be traced, marked, and cut accurately.

Place the template face down on the wrong side of the fabric. If the grain line is marked on the template, be sure to align the mark with the lengthwise or crosswise grain of the fabric. Trace the template accurately and cut exactly on the marked line.

Sewing order

Block assembly diagrams are often used to show how the pieces should be put together. Sew the smallest units together first, progressively forming larger units.

Necessary Notions

Scissors

Use 1 pair of sharp scissors for cutting fabric only and another pair for cutting paper, posterboard, etc.

Needles for hand sewing

Choose regular sewing needles or "sharps," which are especially good for hand appliqué.

Needles for hand quilting

Look for short needles called "betweens." Use the smallest quilting needle that you can thread, because the smaller the needle, the smaller your quilting stitches can be.

Thimble

Worn on the middle finger of the sewing hand, it is essential to protect the finger while hand quilting.

Thread for sewing

Use cotton-covered polyester thread for piecing by hand or by machine.

Thread for hand quilting

You will need 100% cotton or cotton-covered polyester *quilting thread*. Be sure to look for the label that indicates the thread is to be used for quilting.

Thread for machine quilting

Use cotton-covered polyester *sewing thread*. Match the color of the bobbin thread to the color of the quilt backing and the top thread to the quilt top.

Tools for marking fabric for cutting

For marking patterns on light fabrics, use a #2 lead pencil. For dark fabrics, look for special pencils in white, yellow, or silver (available at quilt shops or fabric stores). Any pencil used must sharpen well to produce a thin, clearly visible line.

Tools for marking quilting designs

Marks for *quilting* must be either very light or easily removable. A 0.5mm mechanical pencil with an H or 2H lead will work on light fabrics. A silver Verithin pencil (available at art supply stores) will sharpen well and can be seen on both dark and light fabrics. A special blue water-soluble marker, sold in quilt shops and fabric stores, can be very convenient but should be used with care. Test your fabric first to be certain that the blue marks can be completely removed with plain water. Do not expose the marked fabric to direct sunlight or heat, because heat will make the marks permanent.

Quarter-inch plastic rod (optional)

Often called a rod seamer or a seam guide, this handy tool measures a consistent ¼-inch seam. Align 1 edge of the rod with the cut edge of the fabric. Use the other edge of the rod as a guide for marking the seam line. This marked line can be very helpful to those who are new to patchwork.

Rotary cutter, mat, and acrylic ruler (optional)

The rotary cutter, used with the protective mat and acrylic ruler, has revolutionized quiltmaking by making it possible to cut many layers of fabric at the same time, quickly and accurately. Often it can eliminate the need for tracing templates.

Techniques and Patterns

Rotary Cutting

The rotary cutter (with a mat and straightedge) makes it possible to measure and cut several layers of fabric at once. Pieces can be cut without marking a sewing line or cutting line. This saves time, but it requires absolute accuracy when measuring. And you must always include the ¼" seam allowances on all sides.

With the rotary cutting method, the fabric is first cut into strips. Except for long borders, the strips are cut on the cross grain. These crossgrain strips can then be cut into squares, rectangles, triangles, and other shapes. A number of projects in this book are ideal projects in which to use the rotary cutting method. These projects will give specific dimensions and the number of strips to cut.

Caution! The rotary cutter blade is very sharp. When you buy a cutter, be sure that it has a safety guard. Keep it in the safe position at all times, except when you are actually making a cut, and always make sure that the cutter is out of the reach of children.

Besides the rotary cutter, you will need a special cutting mat that is designed to protect the blade and the cutting surface. The best mat for cutting strips is at least 23" wide and marked with a ruled grid.

You'll also need a thick plastic ruler to measure the strips and serve as a cutting guide. There are many types of quilter's rulers. The best one for cutting strips is 22" to 24" long and marked with ⅛" increments and a 45° angle. A small square ruler is also helpful.

Note: If you are left-handed, you will need to reverse the following instructions.

1. To create a straight edge for cutting, fold your fabric in half lengthwise, matching the selvages. Align the square ruler with the folded edge of the fabric. Place your quilter's ruler to the left of it, as shown in Diagram A. Holding the quilter's ruler in place with your left hand, remove the square ruler. You will cut from the folded edge to the selvage, guiding the cutter away from you along the ruler with a steady rolling motion. You can move your left hand along the ruler as you cut, but you must not change the position of the ruler. *Always keep your fingers away from the edge of the ruler next to the cutter!*

Diagram A:
Finding the Straight Grain

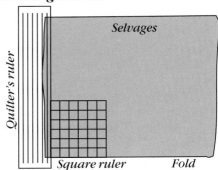

2. The transparent ruler makes it possible to measure and cut at the same time. Fold the fabric in half again, bringing the selvages down to the folded edge. You now have 4 layers of fabric that should line up perfectly along the straight cut you just made. Check the project instructions for the strip width that you will need. Position the ruler to measure the correct distance from your straight-cut edge, as shown in Diagram B. The blade will easily cut through all 4 layers. Unfold the strip, checking to be sure that the cut is straight. The strip length will be the width of the fabric, approximately 44". Using the ruler again, trim away the selvages, cutting off about ½".

Diagram B: Cutting Strips

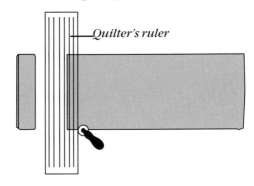

3. Now you can cut squares and rectangles from these strips. Use your small square ruler or quilter's ruler to measure accurately. (See Diagram C.)

Diagram C: Cutting Squares

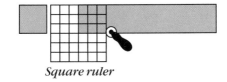

4. You can also use the rotary cutter to cut shapes that require templates. They can be cut more quickly by using the rotary cutter to cut strips the width of the shape (including seam allowances).

Then, using a template, trace the shape onto the fabric and cut the fabric on the marked line with scissors. (See Diagram D.)

Diagram D: Cutting Other Shapes

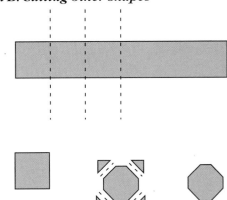

Some projects in this book use the time-saving technique called "strip piecing." With this method, strips are machine-sewn together to make a pieced band. You cut across the seams of the strip-pieced band to make new strips that have alternating fabrics. These new strips can then be assembled to form checkerboards or other designs. This method has become very popular, probably as a result of the rotary cutting revolution.

Cutting Strips With Scissors

People who prefer cutting fabric with scissors can also use the speedy strip-piecing technique. You will need fabric (or dressmaker's) shears that are used only for cutting fabric. They do not have to be expensive, but they must be sharp. You will also need a long quilter's ruler marked in ⅛" increments.

To mark cutting lines on the fabric, *with right sides facing*, fold the fabric in half lengthwise, matching the selvages. Fold it in half again, bringing the folded edge down to the selvages. You will need to mark a straight line from which you can begin to measure the strips, as shown in Diagram A. After removing the square ruler, hold the quilter's ruler firmly and draw a line with a pencil that shows up clearly on the fabric. Use a #2 lead pencil for light fabrics and a white, yellow, or silver pencil for dark fabrics. Start with this line to measure the strip width. Measure and mark the number of strips required. To keep the layers from shifting, pin the fabric in 2 places between the marks.

Cut along each marked line with scissors, using a firm, steady motion. Sharp scissors will easily make a smooth cut through the 4 layers.

Machine Piecing

Quick piecing on the sewing machine is essential to speedy production of items for your bazaar. Your machine does not have to be a new computerized model. A good straight stitch is all that's really necessary, although it can be very helpful if your machine has a zigzag or satin stitch for appliqué. Clean and oil your sewing machine regularly, use good-quality thread, and replace needles frequently.

Accuracy in cutting is very important for successful machine piecing. The cut pieces must include the seam allowance, but the sewing line is not marked on the fabric.

Therefore, a way to achieve a consistent ¼" seam allowance is essential. Many machines have a presser foot that measures ¼" from the edge of the needle to the right edge of the presser foot. Other machines have an adjustable needle that can be set for a ¼" seam. If your machine has neither of these, you will need to experiment to find exactly where the fabric must be placed to achieve the ¼" seam on your machine. Mark that position on the presser foot or throat plate.

Set the stitch length to produce a seam that is strong, but not too difficult to remove with a seam ripper, if necessary. Machines and personal preferences vary, but the best stitch setting is usually 10-12 stitches per inch.

Pin pieces only when it's really necessary. If a straight seam is no longer than about 4" and if this seam does not have to match an adjoining seam, pinning is not necessary. However, when seams must match, it is helpful to align the points that must match and push a pin through the 2 pieces at that point. Turn the pinned unit to the other side to check the alignment; then pin it securely. As you sew the seam, be sure to remove each pin just before the needle reaches it.

Chain piecing saves time. Stack the pieces to be sewn in pairs with right sides facing. Sew the first pair of pieces together, but do not lift the presser foot when you have finished the seam. Do not remove the sewn piece or cut the thread. Just sew 3 or 4 stitches off the fabric and then feed a second pair of pieces into the machine. Continue sewing in this manner until all of the sets have been joined. You will have a chain of pieces, which you can stack until you are ready to clip them apart. (See Diagram A.)

Diagram A: Chain Piecing

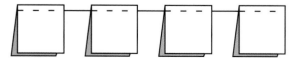

Careful pressing adds to your precision when you are machine-piecing. Do not use a back-and-forth sliding movement. This motion can distort accurately sewn pieces. Instead, use an up-and-down motion to press the seam with the piece flat, just as it comes from the sewing machine. Then open the piece and press the seam allowance toward the darker fabric. Or you can even press the seam open because machine piecing produces a very strong stitch.

Most of the seams for the bazaar projects will be sewn straight across, from raw edge to raw edge. Since they will be crossed by other seams, they will not require any backstitches to secure them. When you are piecing diamonds, parallelograms, or other angled seams, however, you will need to use set-in seams. These take a little longer. It is helpful to mark the corner dots (shown on the templates) on your fabric pieces. A set-in seam will begin or end at that dot, never extending beyond it into the seam allowance. When beginning or ending a seam at the corner dot, always backstitch (sew a few stitches in reverse) to lock the seam.

Because sewing curved seams can be tricky, you will find very few curved seams in the projects in this book. The curves that are necessary are gradual and will probably not require any clipping. If you find that you need a little extra "give," you can prepare the concave (inward) curve by scoring it as shown in Diagram B, Figure 1. With the sharp tips of the scissors, make ⅛" cuts about every ¼" on the concave edge.

Diagram B: Sewing Curves

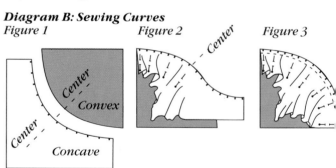

Figure 1   Figure 2   Figure 3

Fold both concave and convex pieces in half to locate and mark the center. Place the 2 pieces with right sides facing and with the concave piece on top. Match the center marks and pin at that point. Then match the edges at which the seam will begin and pin them. Curving the concave edge to align the raw edges, pin the pieces as needed in the interval between the 2 pins, as shown in Figure 2. Match and pin the edges where the seam will end and place pins between them and the center in the same manner. (See Figure 3.) With the concave piece on top, stitch the seam slowly, removing the pins just before the needle reaches them.

Stenciling

You will need:
Sheets of frosted mylar or .005 clear acetate
Masking tape
#2 pencil
Craft knife
Plate glass or other hard cutting surface (the rotary cutter mat is not recommended)
Repositionable spray stencil adhesive
Transparent tape
Acrylic craft or fabric paint
A shallow dish
Stencil brushes or sponges
Paper towels
A smooth, flat surface for stenciling

Prepare the mylar stencils by taping a piece of mylar (frosted side up) over the stencil design. Trace the outline with the pencil. Cut out the design, making a separate stencil for each paint color. (To make alignment easier, trace the entire design on each sheet of mylar, but cut out only those sections to be stenciled in 1 color.) Use clear tape to mend any cutting errors.

Tape the fabric right side up to the smooth work surface. Spray the back of the stencil with reposionable spray stencil adhesive (available in art supply or craft stores) or use masking tape to firmly adhere the stencil to the fabric. Pour a small amount of paint into the shallow dish. Dip the end of the brush into the paint and dab the bristles onto several layers of paper towels to blot the excess paint. The brush should be almost dry so that the paint won't run.

Starting with the largest color area and working with 1 color at a time, work from the outside edge toward the center. The paint should be applied with a light tapping motion, "pouncing" the brush straight up and down. A sponge may be used instead of a brush, for a dappled effect. Dilute the paint slightly with water and dip the sponge in. Squeeze the sponge to distribute the paint evenly and to remove excess paint. Stencil with a light, dabbing motion.

Clean the stencils with a wet paper towel. Allow each color to dry for several hours before applying an additional color, if necessary. Heat-set the designs by pressing on the wrong side of the fabric with a press cloth and a hot, dry iron.

Sponge-Painting

A sponge can be used without a stencil to paint colorful designs. Cut the sponges into the desired shapes, dip into the paint as described above, and with a straight up-and down motion, imprint the shape of the sponge on fabric or paper.

Easy Appliqué

With appliqué, the designs are cut out and stitched (applied) to a background fabric. We've selected some of the fastest appliqué methods for making bazaar projects, and you can use the same methods for making quick gifts and quilts.

Paper-backed Fusible Web

Fusing cutout designs to a background fabric is easy, even for beginners, and it's superfast because there is no seam allowance to turn under. Follow the manufacturer's directions for a "permanent bond," to ensure that the appliqués will adhere even after washing.

Following the manufacturer's instructions, fuse the web to the wrong side of the appliqué fabric. Then trace the template on the paper backing. (If the template is asymmetrical, turn the template over and trace it face down on the paper backing.) Cut out the paper-backed fabric shape on the outline. Peel away the paper backing. Place the shape, web side down, on the right side of the background fabric and fuse it in place.

Machine Appliqué

For machine appliqué, no seam allowances are required. Use fusible web to adhere the appliqué pieces to the background fabric. Place a piece of lightweight paper or tear-away stabilizer beneath the background fabric behind the appliqué shape. Using a matching or a contrasting thread, finish the edges of the appliqué shapes with a machine-satin stitch (a close-spaced zigzag). Test your stitch length and width by sewing a sample first.

Freezer Paper Hand Appliqué

Hand appliqué is the best way to achieve the look of traditional appliqué, although it takes longer than the methods described above because there is a seam allowance to turn under. However, using freezer paper, which is sold in the grocery store, can save a lot of time because it eliminates the need for hand basting the seam allowance.

Appliqué templates are made with no seam allowance. Trace the template onto the *dull* side of the freezer paper and cut the paper on the marked line. Make a freezer paper shape for each piece to be appliquéd. Pin the freezer paper shape, with its *shiny side up,* to the *wrong side* of your fabric. Following the paper shape and adding a scant ¼" seam allowance, cut out the fabric piece. Do not remove the pins.

Diagram A: Pressing Points

Figure 1

Wrong side of fabric

Shiny side of freezer paper

Figure 2

Figure 3

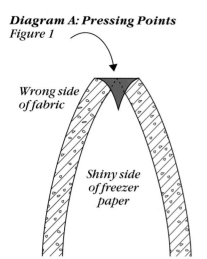
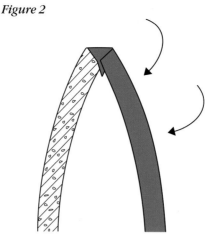
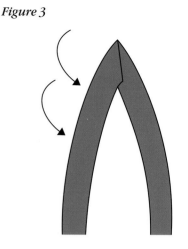

Seam allowances are not basted, as in traditional appliqué. You use the tip of a hot, *dry* iron to press the seam allowance to the shiny side of the freezer paper. (Be careful not to touch the shiny side of the freezer paper with the iron.)

Shapes with points require special attention and should be pressed first. Turn the fabric down at the point and press it. (See Diagram A, Figure 1.) Fold the seam allowance on 1 side over the point and press it (see Figure 2); then fold the seam allowance on the other side over the point and press it. (See Figure 3.)

When pressing curved edges, you may find it necessary to clip sharp inward curves, as shown in Diagram B. If the shape doesn't curve smoothly, separate the paper from the fabric with your fingernail, and try again. Practice will make this process easier.

Diagram B: Curved Shapes

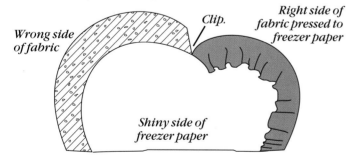

Wrong side of fabric

Clip.

Right side of fabric pressed to freezer paper

Shiny side of freezer paper

It isn't necessary to turn under any seam allowances that will be covered by another appliqué piece.

Remove the pins when all of the seam allowances have been pressed to the freezer paper. Position the prepared appliqué piece right side up on your background fabric. Press to adhere it to the background fabric. A large appliqué piece should probably be pinned in place as well, to make it very secure.

The appliqué is now ready to be stitched in place. Use a single strand of cotton-wrapped polyester sewing thread in a color that matches the appliqué piece, not the background fabric. You may use a slipstitch or a blindstitch, but keep the stitch very small on the top surface. Don't be concerned if you catch a bit of the freezer paper in the stitches.

To remove the freezer paper after your stitching is complete, cut away the background fabric behind the appliqué piece, leaving ¼" seam allowances. Now you won't have to quilt through an extra layer. Separate the freezer paper from the fabric with your fingernail and pull gently to remove it.

If you prefer not to cut away the background fabric, leave 1½" unstitched when stitching the appliqué piece to the background fabric. Reach in with your fingernail or a pin and separate the fabric from the freezer paper. Gently pull the paper out. Turning under the seam allowance as you go, close the opening with appliqué stitches.

Embroidery Stitches

Running Stitch
Make stitches, leaving even, stitch-length spaces between them.

Backstitch
Bring the needle up at the right end of the design. Reinsert the needle to the right and bring it up again to the left of the place where thread emerged. Repeat, making even stitches.

Satin Stitch
Bring the needle up on 1 side of design and make a stitch to the opposite side of the design. Slide the needle under the fabric and repeat, keeping the stitches flat.

Diagram A: Chainstitch Figure 1

Figure 2

Chainstitch
Bring the thread up and make a loop as shown in Diagram A, Figure 1. Holding the loop close to the fabric with the left thumb, insert the needle again as close as possible to the place where the thread first emerged. Re-insert the needle a short distance away to start the next stitch. Do not pull the loops tight. (See Figure 2.)

Lazy Daisy Stitch
Make a single chainstitch. When a loop is formed, take a small stitch at the center of the loop, and bring the thread out at the beginning of the next loop.

Diagram B: French Knot Figure 1

Figure 2

Figure 3

French Knot
Bring the needle up where the knot is to be. Holding the thread in your left hand, wrap around the point of the needle 2 or 3 times as shown in Diagram, B, Figure 1. Holding the loops in place with your left hand, re-insert needle as close as possible to where the thread first emerged. (See Figure 2.) Pull the needle through the loops to the wrong side of the fabric, forming 1 small round stitch. (See Figure 3.)

Blanket Stitch
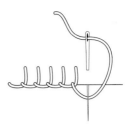

Working from left to right, bring the needle up on the bottom edge of the design. Insert the needle above and to the right of the starting point. Keeping the thread behind the needle point, bring the needle out at the edge of the design.

Yo-Yos

Referring to the project instructions for size, make a circle template from pattern on page 157. Trace the circle on the *right* side of the fabric. Cut the fabric ¼" outside of the marked line. Referring to the Diagram, Figure 1, turn the seam allowance under on the marked line as you take small running stitches through both layers of fabric. Run this gathering thread all the way around the circle. (See Figure 2.) Pull the thread tightly to gather the edges to the center. (See Figure 3.) Secure the thread with a knot and clip it. Distribute the gathers evenly and press the circle flat.

Diagram: Making Yo-Yos:
Figure 1

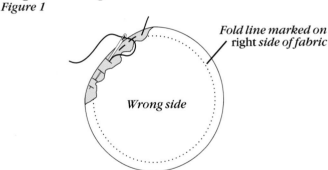

Fold line marked on right side of fabric

Wrong side

Figure 2

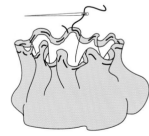

Figure 3

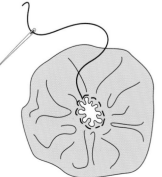

Fabric Rosebuds

Referring to your project instructions, select the correct circle pattern from page 157. Make a template and cut a circle from fabric. Referring to the Diagram, Figure 1, with wrong sides facing, fold the fabric circle in half. Beginning at the left side, turn the folded edge down at an angle and pin. (See Figure 2.)

Now turn the half-circle over, so that the angled fold is face down. Fold the right side in, as shown in Figure 3; then fold the left side over the folded right edge. (See Figure 4.)

Referring to Figure 5, run a gathering thread along the raw edges. Remove pin. Pull to gather. Knot the thread to secure it.

Diagram: Making Rosebuds

Figure 1

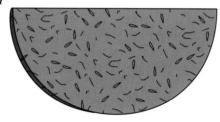

Figure 2

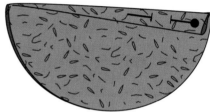

Figure 3

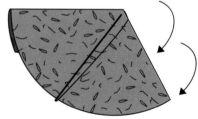

Figure 4

Figure 5

Bias Strips for Stems

Purchased ¼" double-fold bias tape can be used for making stems for appliqué, but if you prefer to make your own bias stems, here are 2 easy methods. Both techniques begin with 1"-wide strips cut on the bias. Cut the strips a little longer than the length you want the stems to be.

Folded Bias Stems

Folded stems are easy to make because they do not require any stitching. With the right side down, fold 1 long edge up ⅓ of the way and press. Fold the other long edge down over the first, stopping just before the raw edge meets the pressed fold. Press. (See Diagram A.) Appliqué with the raw edge facing the background fabric.

Diagram A: Folded Stem

Bias Bar Stems

For a bias bar stem, purchase ¼" bias bars from a quilt shop or fabric store. With right sides facing, fold the bias strip in half lengthwise and stitch it along the folded edge with a ¼" seam. Trim the seam to ⅛". Insert the bias bar into the fabric tube and center the seam. (See Diagram B.) Leaving the bias bar inside the fabric, steam-press both sides of the fabric tube, pressing the seam allowance to 1 side. Allow the strip to cool before removing the bias bar. Appliqué with the raw edges of the seam facing the background fabric.

Diagram B: Bias Bar Stem

Borders

Instructions for all projects that require borders specify whether the border strips will abut at the corners or the corners will be mitered at a 45° angle. Measurements for border strips will be given. Whenever possible, borders should be cut from the lengthwise grain of the fabric.

Straight Borders

Side borders are added first. (See Diagram A, Figure 1.) With right sides facing and raw edges aligned, pin the center of 1 border strip to the center of 1 side of the quilt. Pin the border to the quilt at each end and then place pins along the side at intervals. Machine-stitch with the border strip on top. Press the seam toward the border. Add the border to the other side and then the top and bottom borders in the same manner. (See Figure 2.)

Diagram A:
Straight Borders
Figure 1

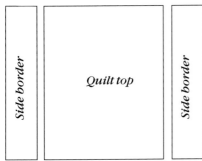

Figure 2

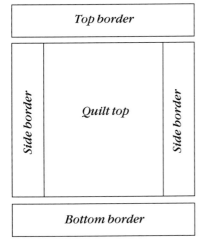

Mitered Borders

1. With right sides facing and raw edges aligned, center 1 border strip on 1 side of the quilt top. Pin the border at the center and ¼" from each end of the quilt top (border fabric will extend beyond these pins). Pin the border at intervals between. Start stitching at the outermost pin, backstitching to lock the stitches. Continue to sew until you reach the last pin. Stop and backstitch again. Join the remaining borders in the same manner.

Diagram B:
Mitered Borders
Figure 1

Figure 2

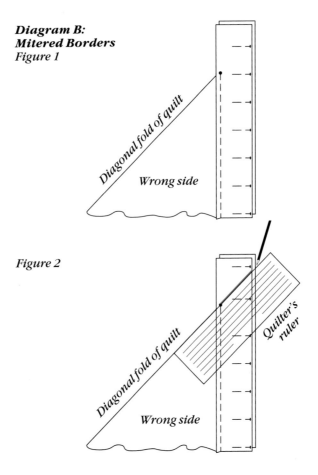

2. With right sides facing, fold the quilt diagonally, aligning the raw edges of 2 adjacent borders. Pin securely. (See Diagram B, Figure 1.)
3. Align a yardstick or quilter's ruler along the diagonal fold, as shown in Figure 2. Holding the ruler firmly, mark a line from the place where the stitching ended to the outer edge of the border.
4. Start machine-stitching exactly at the beginning of the marked line, backstitch, and then stitch on the line out to the raw edge.
5. Unfold the quilt to be sure that the corner lies flat, and correct the stitching if necessary. Trim the seam to ¼".
6. Miter the 3 remaining corners in the same manner. Press the corner seams open and press the border seams toward the borders.

Basting with Safety Pins

Machine quilters prefer basting with safety pins because there are no basting threads to get caught on the presser foot, but it is also a fast way to baste projects to be tied or hand-quilted. Although finishing techniques will vary for different projects, the following are general directions for most quilted items.

Press the quilt top and the backing. Mark the quilting design on the quilt top. Place the backing, *right side down,* on a smooth surface. (Be sure to work on a surface that won't be harmed by pin scratches.) Use masking tape on the edges in several places to hold it smooth. Then add the batting and the marked quilt top, *right side up.*

The best pin to use is a #1 nickel-plated safety pin, but for a thick batting, you may need the larger #2 pins. Insert the pins through all 3 layers, lifting the quilt as little as possible.

For a tied quilt or hand-quilted project, you'll need to place pins at approximately 6" intervals. For machine quilting, pins should be placed at 4" intervals. Starting in the center and working toward the outside edges, place pins along vertical and horizontal lines (See Diagram, Figure 1.) Avoid the marked quilting lines and seams. Working out from the center, place additional pins at intervals, forming a grid, as shown in Figure 2.

Diagram: Pin Placement

Figure 1

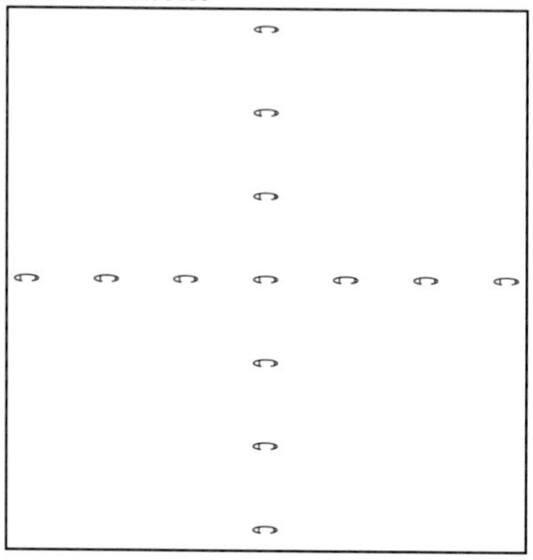

Figure 2

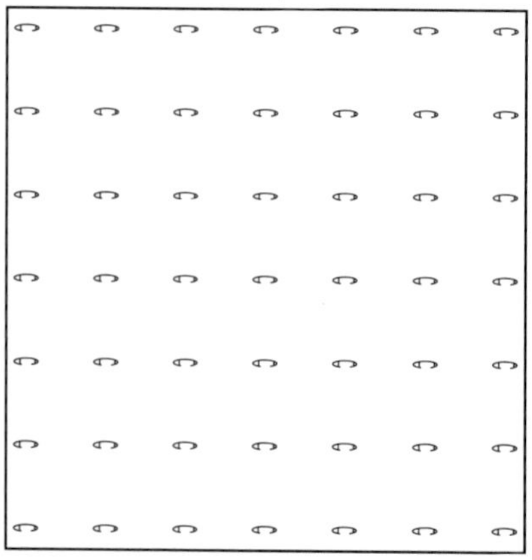

A project that is to be machine-quilted will require more pinning. (The more pins you have the patience to use, the smoother your machine quilting will be.) The pins should be no farther than 4" apart and should not be placed on the seams or on the marked quilting lines. This should keep you from having to remove any pins as you machine-quilt.

Tying Quilts

Tying is the fastest way to secure the 3 quilt layers. It is the only way to work with the thick batting that is most often used for comforters. Colorful ties can also add special decorative effects to the overall design of your projects.

Ties can be pearl cotton, synthetic yarn, ribbon floss, or narrow ribbon. The material used for ties should be strong enough to be tied very tightly and stay tied. Ties may be double knots, bows, pom-poms, or knots that hold buttons, charms, or beads. *Never use buttons or other small objects on quilts for babies or small children.*

Ties should be placed at least every 6", avoiding the places where seams are joined. You will need a sharp embroidery needle with an eye large enough to accommodate the tie material that you have chosen.

Thread the needle but do not knot the thread end. Starting in the center of your basted quilt top, take a ⅛" to ¼" stitch through all 3 layers. Clip the thread, leaving a tail of thread several inches long on each side of the stitch. Tie the 2 tails in a tight double knot. Trim the tails of all the knots to the same length.

If you want to tie bows, leave longer tails and tie the double knot first; then tie the tails in a bow. Now tie the loops of the bow in a knot to be sure that the knot is very secure.

Although wide ribbon can be too difficult to pull through all 3 layers, wide ribbon bows can look as if they have been tied. Cut the ribbon in 12" lengths and then tie it into bows. With sewing thread that matches the color of the bows, hand-sew the bows in place. (Make sure that your stitches go through all 3 layers.)

Bows and buttons may also be attached by sewing machine, using a zigzag stitch. The stitch must be set wide enough so that the needle "jumps" over the center of the button or over the knot of a tied ribbon bow. Start and stop these stitches by using a straight stitch to take a few stitches in place to secure the threads. If your sewing machine makes decorative stitches, you may want to use them to create a machine-tied quilt, by placing decorative stitches at the intervals where the ties would be.

Hand Quilting

Most of these bazaar projects can easily be quilted by machine. However, you may want to hand-quilt a few smaller projects if time permits. Use a thin polyester batting for pieces that are to be hand-quilted. You will need a single 18" length of quilting thread. For short stitches, use the smallest needle possible. Beginners should probably begin with a size 8 or 9 "between" needle and gradually work up to a size 11 or 12. You may quilt without a hoop or frame, if the piece is well-basted. If you prefer to use a hoop, adjust the hoop tension so that there is a little "give" in the quilt top.

To begin stitching, make a small knot about 1" away from the end of the thread. Insert the threaded needle into the quilt top and batting about 1" away from where the first quilting stitch will be and take a long stitch. (See Diagram A, Figure 1.) The thread should not go through to the backing. Tug the thread gently through the top until the knot is buried in the batting. (See Figure 2.)

Diagram A:
Starting Stitching
Figure 1

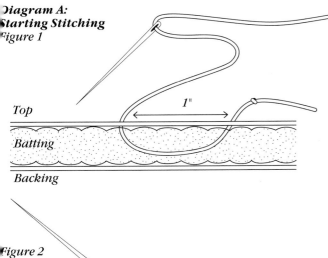

Top

Batting

Backing

Figure 2

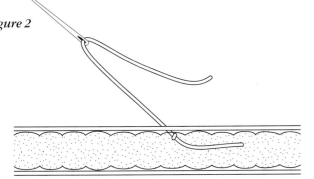

After the knot is buried in the batting, make small, even running stitches through all 3 layers of the quilt, as shown in Diagram B. To protect your finger from injury, wear a thimble on the middle finger of your quilting hand.

Diagram B:
Quilting Stitch

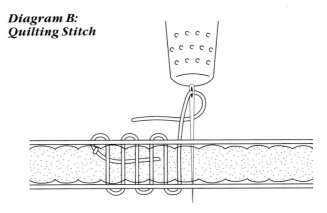

To end the stitching, bring the thread to the surface just past the last stitch. With the needle still threaded, form the thread into a circle and pass the needle under the loop the thread has formed. Hold the thread as shown in Diagram C, Figure 1, and pull the loop tight. A small knot will form in the quilting thread close to the surface of the quilt top. Reinsert the needle into the hole where the thread came out (see Figure 2), and run the needle under the top layer, into the batting for about 1". Do not go through to the backing. Bring the needle back up through the quilt top about 1" away. Tug the thread gently to pull the knot under the quilt top and into the batting. Clip the thread at the surface.

Diagram C: Ending Stitching
Figure 1

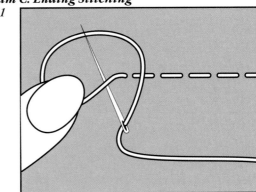

Figure 2

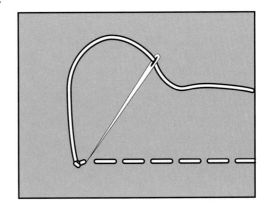

Machine Quilting

The speed of machine quilting is ideal for making bazaar projects. The small size of most of these projects makes it very easy to manipulate them through the machine, and they can be quickly quilted using straight-line machine quilting. Try a very small project or a practice piece first.

Machine quilting stitches can match the back of the quilt as well as the front. Fill your bobbin with cotton-covered polyester sewing thread (not quilting thread) in a color that matches the back of your project. Thread the machine itself with the same type of thread, in a color that will match or coordinate with your project's colors. (There is a very fine nylon thread available for machine quilting, but we do not recommend it for these projects unless you are experienced with its use.)

An even-feed or walking foot is designed to feed all the layers of your project through the machine at the same speed. It is possible to machine-quilt without this special foot (by experimenting with tension adjustments and presser foot pressure), but it will be much easier *with* it. If your machine does not have this foot, check with your sewing machine dealer to find a foot that will work on your machine.

If your project is large, roll the 2 opposite sides toward the center. Leave a large center section open and secure the rolled sides with bicycle clips. These metal bands are available in quilt shops and many fabric stores, as well as in bicycle shops.

Start stitching in the top center. Begin by stitching in place several times to lock your stitches; or you may begin with a very short stitch and sew for about ½", gradually increasing the length to a setting of 8 to 10 stitches per inch.

The easiest method for machine quilting is quilting "in-the-ditch" (stitching done just beside the seam lines). The seam lines for the blocks and sashing form a grid across the length and width of the quilt. These will be the longest lines of quilting, and they should always be done first.

Quilt down the center, from 1 edge to the other. If you started your first quilting row at the top, begin the next row of quilting at the bottom. (Alternating the direction of the center quilting lines will keep the layers from shifting.) Continue quilting ½ of the quilt, unrolling as you go until you reach the edge. Remove the quilt from the sewing machine and re-roll the completed side of the quilt. Turn the quilt and work out from the center again to complete the quilting lines on the other side of the quilt.

When you have completed the vertical quilting lines, unroll the quilt and reroll it in the other direction to quilt the horizontal lines. Start in the center and proceed in the manner above.

Some projects do not have quilting lines that form a vertical and horizontal grid. The lines may form a diagonal grid or follow the design of the patchwork pattern. Always stitch the longest lines of the quilting first, starting in the center.

Because beginning and ending machine stitches show on the back of the quilt, nonstop quilting diagrams are given for projects whenever possible. Follow the arrows on the diagram, pivoting with the needle down to change the direction of the stitching.

Binding

Since these projects were designed for ease and speed of assembly, purchased bias tape is an excellent choice for binding. However, when it is not possible to find exactly the color you want, it may be necessary to make your own. Straight-grain binding is easy to make and will work well on any item with straight sides. This technique for applying the pieced binding creates self-mitering corners on right-angled pieces, such as wall quilts.

We recommend a double-layer binding. Double-layer binding wears well and can be applied quickly. Strips cut 2" wide will yield a finished binding that measures ⅜". If you are working with very thick batting or if you prefer a wider binding, you may want to use strips cut 3¼" wide for a ⅝"-wide finished binding.

The length of the binding strip should equal the perimeter measurement of the project plus 12". Border strips can be pieced from cross-grain strips. (This is the most economical use of your fabric.) Refer to Diagram A for making angled seams, which will lie smoother than straight seams when the binding is folded over. After the entire length of fabric needed for the binding has been pieced, fold the strip in half lengthwise, with wrong sides facing, and press it.

Diagram A: Pieced Binding

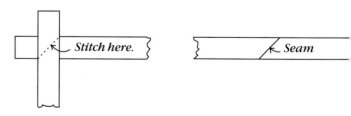

The binding is applied to the front of the quilt first. You may begin anywhere on the edge of the quilt, except at the corner.

1. Lay the binding along the raw edge of the quilt. Referring to Diagram B, Figure 1, fold down the top corner of the binding at a 45° angle, align the raw edges, and pin.

2. Beginning at the folded end, machine-stitch the binding to the quilt, using a ¼" seam. At the corner, stop stitching ¼" from the edge. Backstitch, clip the threads, and remove the quilt from the sewing machine. Turn the quilt ¼ turn and fold the binding strip diagonally away from the quilt, creating a 45° angle. (See Figure 2.)

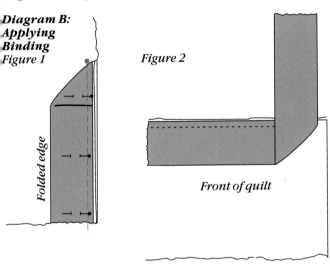

Diagram B: Applying Binding
Figure 1   Figure 2

Folded edge

Front of quilt

3. Now fold the binding strip straight down along the next side to be stitched, creating a pleat in the corner. Place your sewing machine needle just at the ¼" seam line of the new side. (See Figure 3.) Make a few stitches, backstitch to secure, and then stitch the length of the seam. Stop stitching at the corner, ¼" from the edge. Continue until all 4 sides of the binding have been joined to the quilt, overlapping the end of the binding strip over the beginning fold and stitching about 2" beyond it. Trim the excess binding strip.

Figure 3

Machine stitching begins here.

Front of quilt

Turn the folded edge of the binding to the back of the quilt and slipstitch it in place, using a thread that matches the binding. The folded edge at the beginning of the binding strip will create a neat, angled edge when the strip is folded to the back. (See Figure 4.) Stop when you reach the corner seam and fold the corner to form a miter. (See Figure 5.) The binding will form a mitered fold on the front side as well. Continue stitching, forming mitered folds on all 4 corners. You may hand-stitch the miters closed if desired.

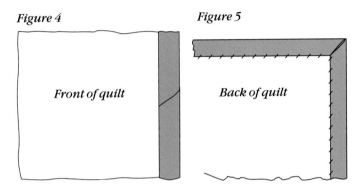

Figure 4   Figure 5

Front of quilt   Back of quilt

Hanging Sleeve

Quilts that are to be hung for wall display should have a sleeve for hanging attached to the back. A dowel or curtain rod can be slipped through the sleeve and hung from brackets on the wall. Cut a 6"-wide piece of muslin that measures the width of the quilt plus 2". To hem the ends, turn under ¼" on each end and press. Turn under an additional 1" on each end, press, and topstitch. With wrong sides facing and raw edges aligned, stitch the long edges together. Center the seam in the muslin tube and press the seam open. Referring to the Diagram, with the seam facing the back of the quilt, place the top of the sleeve about 1" below the binding of the top of the quilt; center the sleeve between the sides of the quilt. Slipstitch the top and bottom edges of the sleeve to the quilt backing only, making sure that no stitches go through to the quilt top.

Diagram: Hanging Sleeve

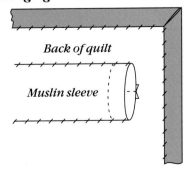

Back of quilt

Muslin sleeve

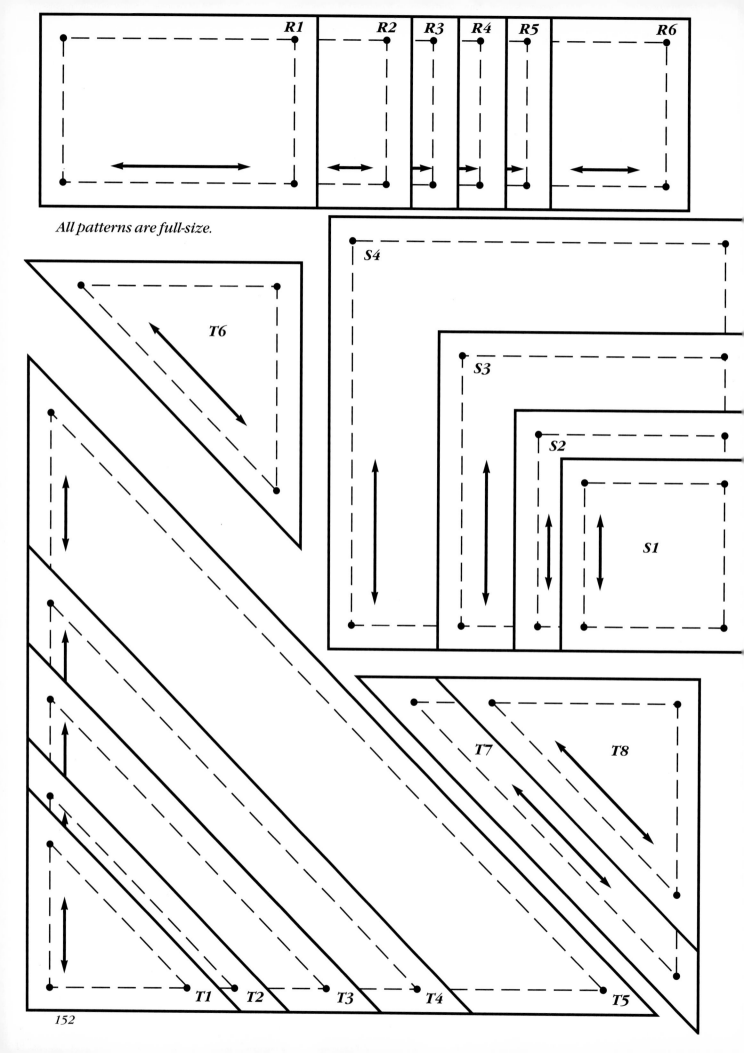

R1 R2 R3 R4 R5 R6

All patterns are full-size.

T6

S4

S3

S2

S1

T7 T8

T1 T2 T3 T4 T5

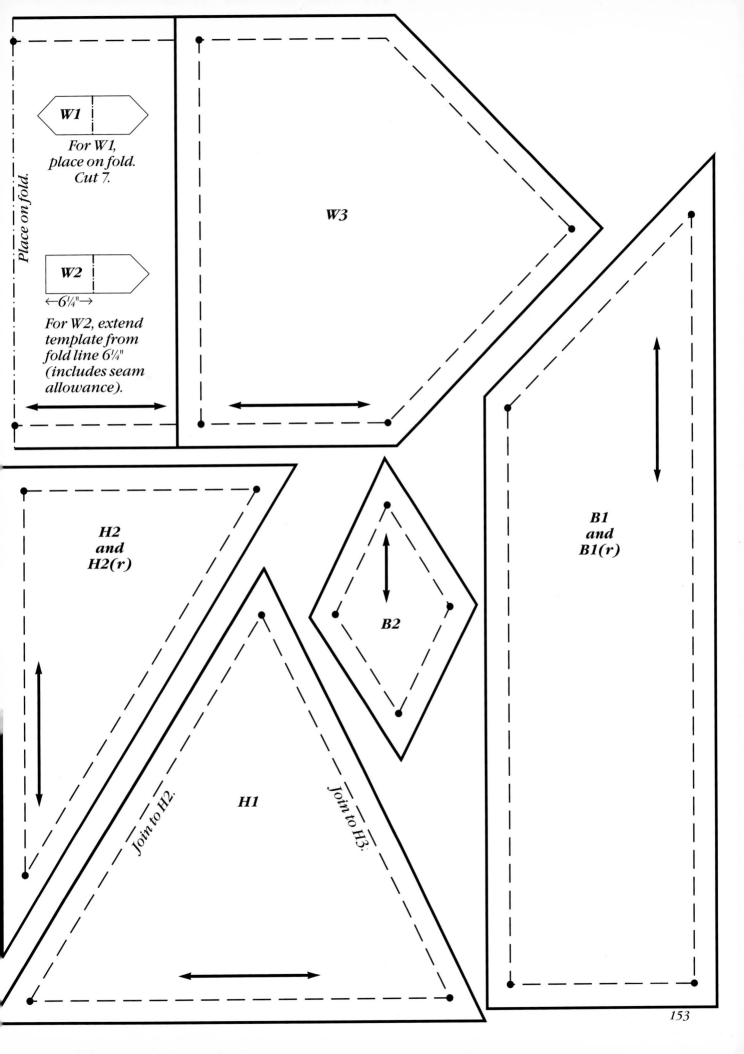

W1

For W1,
place on fold.
Cut 7.

Place on fold.

W2

←6¼"→

For W2, extend
template from
fold line 6¼"
(includes seam
allowance).

W3

B1
and
B1(r)

H2
and
H2(r)

B2

Join to H2.

H1

Join to H3.

153

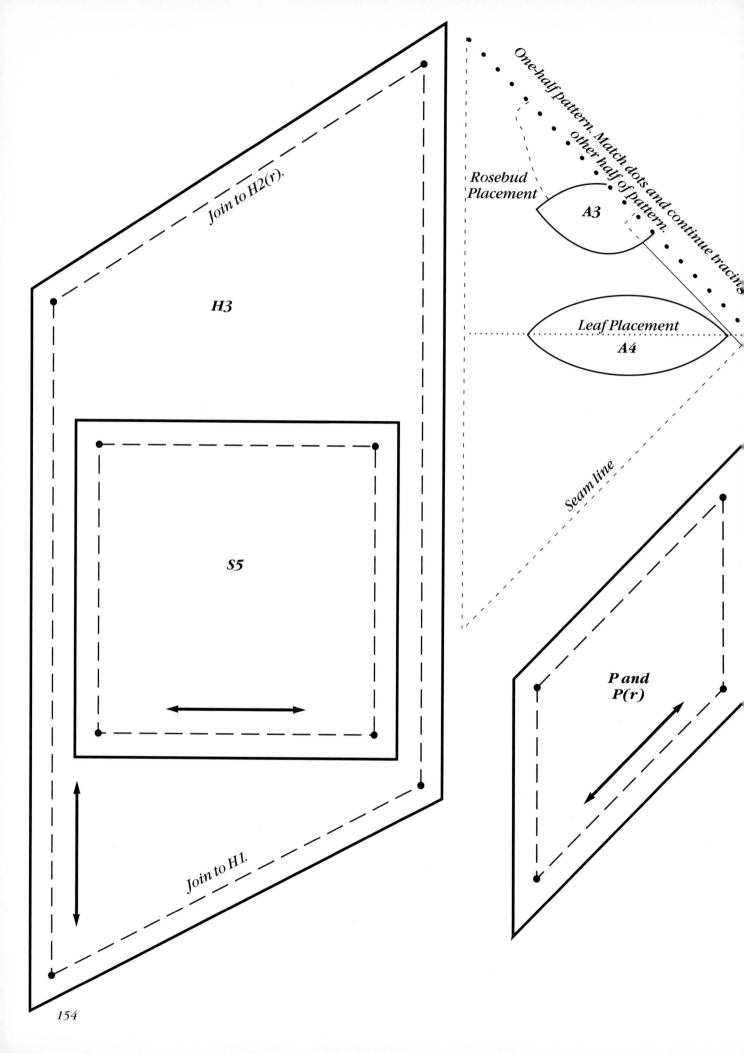

Join to H2(r).

H3

One-half Pattern. Match dots and continue tracing other half of pattern.

Rosebud Placement

A3

Leaf Placement

A4

Seam line

S5

P and P(r)

Join to H1.

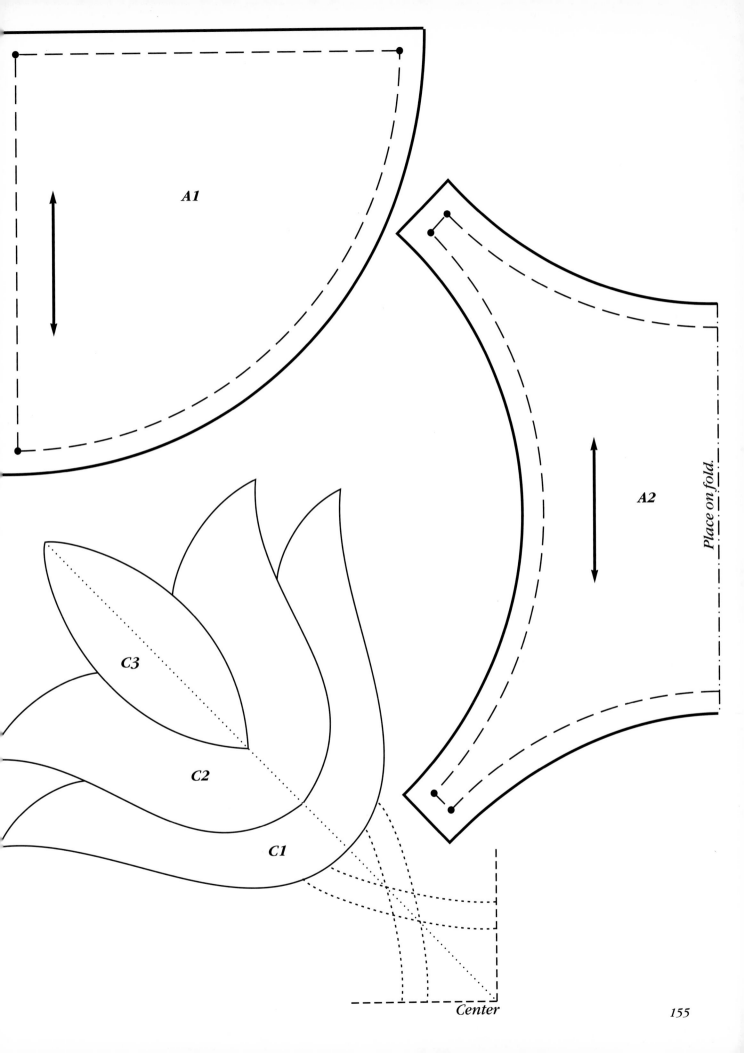

A1

A2

Place on fold.

C3

C2

C1

Center

155

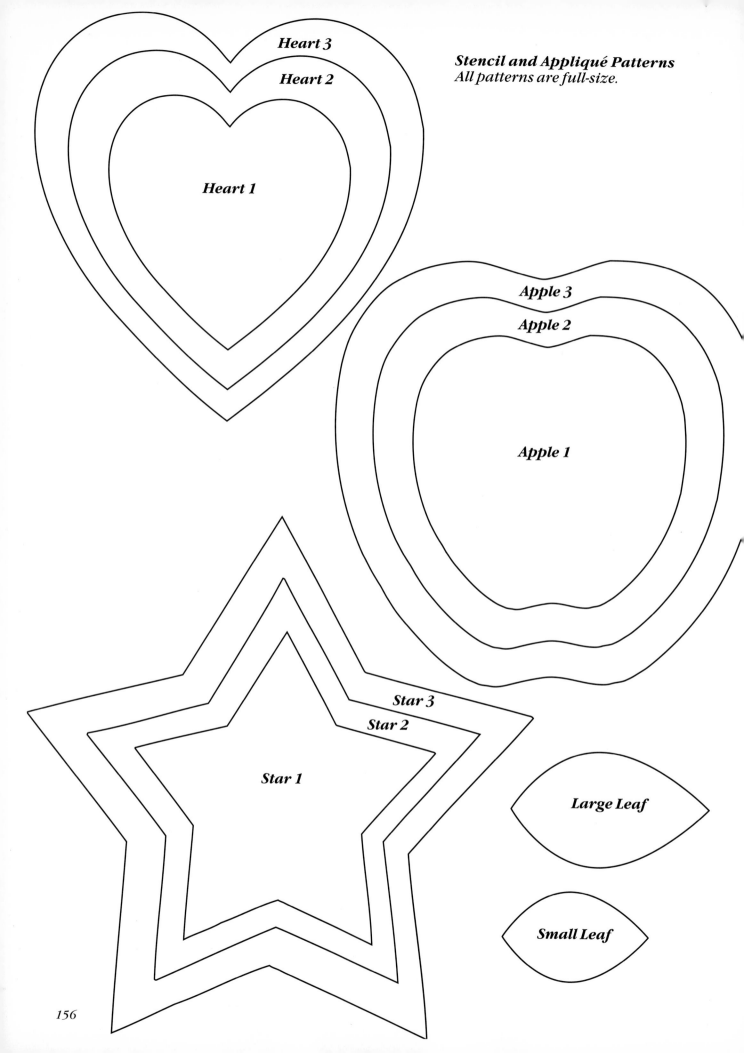

Heart 3

Heart 2

Heart 1

Stencil and Appliqué Patterns
All patterns are full-size.

Apple 3

Apple 2

Apple 1

Star 3

Star 2

Star 1

Large Leaf

Small Leaf

156

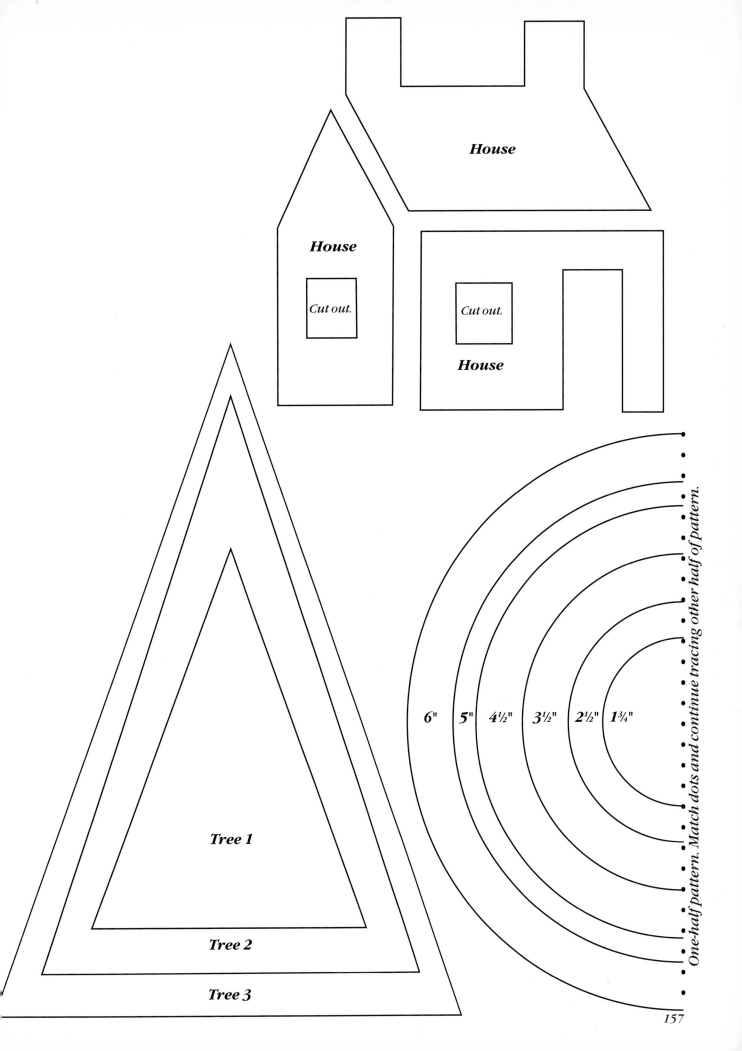

House

House

Cut out.

Cut out.

House

Tree 1

Tree 2

Tree 3

6"   5"   4½"   3½"   2½"   1¾"

One-half pattern. Match dots and continue tracing other half of pattern.

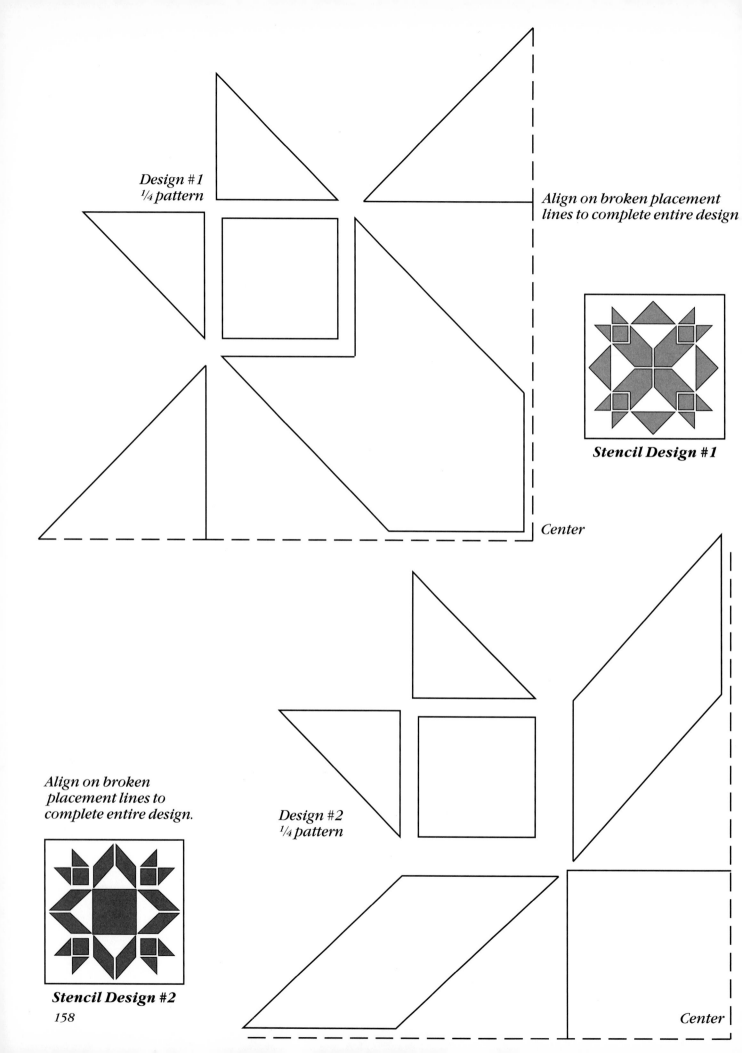

Design #1
¼ pattern

Align on broken placement lines to complete entire design

Stencil Design #1

Center

Align on broken placement lines to complete entire design.

Design #2
¼ pattern

Stencil Design #2

Center

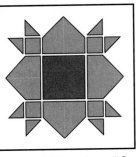

Stencil Design #3

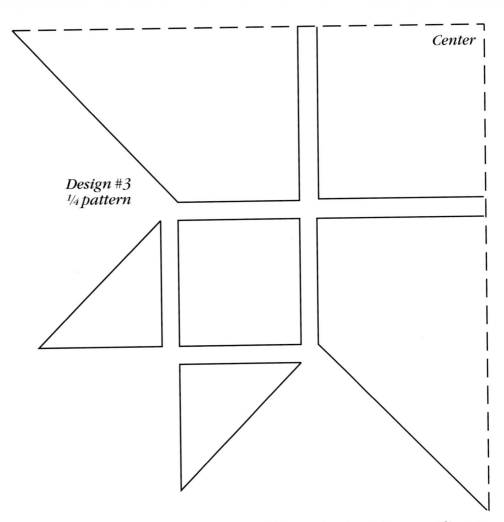

Center

Design #3
¼ pattern

Align on broken placement lines to complete entire design.

Designers and Contributors

Barbara Ball, Bazaar Banner, pages 130–131; Bazaar Price Tags, page 132.

Ginger Kean Berk, Sunbonnet Sam Set, pages 64–69; assisted by Barbara Einhorn; fabrics by Concord; batting by Mountain Mist; thread by Wrights Mettler Swiss Metrosene Plus and Mettler Embroidery Thread; Stitch-n-Tear stabilizer and Wonder-Under fusible web by Freudenberg Non-Wovens Limited Partnership; yarn by Spinrite Yarns & Dyers Limited.
Note: Ginger Kean Berk's *Sunbonnet Sue* quilt and accessories can be found in *Quick Quilts*, published by Oxmoor House, Inc.

Judith M. Biber, Flower Garden and Soccer Star Sweatshirts, pages 57–58; Party Bibs for Boys and Girls, pages 71–73; Animal Pal Bibs, pages 76–79.

Arleen Boyd, Little Chef Apron, pages 31–32; *Ohio Star Wall Quilt*, pages 106–108; Armchair Sewing Caddy, page 109.

Judy Cantwell, Patchwork Pillow with Ruffle, page 16; Mock Double Ruffle Pillow, page 17; Pillow with Flanged Border, page 17.

Patricia Ramey Channell, *Star Harvest Sampler* quilt (piecing and quilting), pages 8–13.

Marilyn Dorwart, Candy Cane Party Mats, pages 86–87.

Betsy Freeman, Pretty Bows for Girls, page 47.

Betsy Freeman and Don Tyler, Siamese Cat Belt, pages 54–56.

Donna Gallagher, Teatime Table Set, page 22–24; Tulip Table Runner, pages 25–27.

Joyce M. Gillis, Apple Garland, pages 100–101.

Roslyn Oneille Hardy, Easy Doll Quilts, pages 52–54.

Barbara Hendrick, *Star Harvest Sampler* quilt (design), pages 8–13; Elegant Folded Bags (design), pages 110–112; Country Christmas Calicoes (design), pages 98–103.

Pamela Houk, Lollipops and Candy Canes, pages 82–85.

Kindred Spirits (Sally Korte, Alice Strebel), Vintage Accessories, pages 121–125.

Kindred Spirits (Suellen Cochrane Wassem), Antique Sewing Set, pages 113–117.

Cleo Le Vally, Seminole Patchwork Shower Wraps, pages 118–120.

Joan McGlaughlin, Grand Prize Quilt, pages 136–138.

Judy Matthews, Stenciled Crib Quilt, pages 74–75.

Mary E. Ramey, *Star Harvest Sampler* quilt (quilting), pages 8–13.

Radine Robinson, Patchwork Tree Skirt, pages 102–103.

Carol Singletary, Executive Chef Apron, pages 30, 32–33.

Debra Steinmann, Machine Quilted Pot Holders, page 20–21; Rosebud Lingerie Bag, page 110–112.

Carol M. Tipton, Schoolhouse Art Caddy, pages 42–44; Storyteller Apron, pages 48–51.

Sue von Jentzen, Charming Calico Ornaments, pages 90–93.

Eileen Westfall, Quick Lace Kitchen Set, page 28.

Priscilla Wentworth, Patchwork Cap, pages 57, 59–63.

Wild Goose Chase (Susan Rand, Paula Kemperman), Blue Jeans Tote Bags, pages 36–39.

Cecily Zerega, Stenciled Hot Mats, page 29; Stenciled Tote, page 36; Music Box Ornaments, pages 88–90; Hearts and Flowers Stocking and Tree Skirt, pages 94–97; Scrappy Fabric Bows, pages 134–135.

Special thanks to Barbara and Charlie Money, of Irondale, Alabama, and to Diana and Marcus Sullivan and John Tingley, of Springville, Alabama, for allowing us to use their property for production of the photography in this book.

LEISURE ARTS ®

$14.95
100327

ISBN 0-8487-1172-6

7 49075 00327 0